REWIRED: A JOURNEY THROUGH SPARK, SYNTAX, AND STEM

SHAHISTHA TABBASUM

To my beloved grandmother, whose quiet strength, storytelling, and unconditional love still echo in everything I do—you were my first example of resilience and grace.

To my mother, my constant pillar—your courage, your belief in me, and the way you led by example have shaped my journey more than words can ever capture. Every page of this book carries your imprint.

And to all the remarkable women in STEM—past, present, and those yet to come—your brilliance, determination, and quiet revolutions have paved the way for dreamers like me. May this book be a small tribute to your enduring legacy, and an invitation for every young girl to take her place in the lab, in the code, in the sky.

Contents

A woman educator's transformation through the circuits of technology,
the language of logic, and the heart of a classroom.

Acknowledgements

To my dear parents—thank you for being my first teachers. Your unwavering faith in me, your sacrifices, and the values you instilled have been my foundation. Every step I've taken is rooted in your love and support.

To my husband—your patience, strength, and constant encouragement carried me through moments when I doubted myself. You believed in this book before I did, and your quiet confidence became my anchor.

To my children—thank you for being my greatest inspiration. Your questions, your wonder, and the way you look at the world keep me grounded in purpose. This book is for the future you will inherit—and help shape.

To my students, past and present—your curiosity, courage, and even your frustrations have taught me more than any textbook ever could. You rewired my thinking as much as I hoped to rewire yours.

To Ms. Lekshmy Sesha Iyer and Ms. Priyadarshini Narayanan—thank you for being my guiding lights. In the middle of chaos, when I struggled to balance creativity with curriculum, your empathy, wisdom, and practical advice helped me find my rhythm. Your friendship and mentorship have been one of the greatest gifts on this journey.

This book is a tapestry of every conversation, every challenge, and every triumph shared with all of you. Thank you for walking beside me.

Preface

"Technology will never replace great teachers, but technology in the hands of great teachers can be transformational."
— *George Couros*

If you had asked me during my engineering days what I would become, I would have said something about coding, systems architecture, or maybe cybersecurity. Teaching? That wasn't even in the peripherals.

But life has a strange way of rewiring our purpose.

This book is not a manual. It's a memoir. A reflection. A journey and a practical guide. It's about choosing chalk over code — and then learning how to blend both. It's about finding meaning in the unexpected and turning what felt like a detour into my life's direction.

In these pages, you'll find stories — real, raw, sometimes messy — about shifting careers, finding voice, building STEM pathways for the next generation, and refusing to be boxed in by expectations. You'll meet sparks, syntax, struggles, and breakthroughs. It's about the transformation of an educator—of **rewiring** the way I saw teaching, learning, and myself. It's about the **spark** that ignites a child's curiosity, the **syntax** that powers problem-solving, and the rich world of **STEM** that bridges creativity with logic.

As a woman in educational technology, I also write this for every girl who felt out of place in a robotics lab, and every teacher who hesitated before logging into a new platform. This book is a mirror and a map. It's the real story behind the polished lesson plans—the failures, experiments, and lightbulb moments that rewired both my classroom and my career.

Whether you're a teacher, a techie, a student, or simply someone standing at a crossroads, I hope this book reminds you: sometimes, getting rewired is how we find our true circuit.

Welcome to my journey.

CHAPTER ONE

FROM CHALK DUST TO CLICKS

"Somewhere between helping friends pass exams and choosing a career, I discovered I was meant to teach."

From Chalk Dust to Clicks – My early teaching years

I didn't plan to become a teacher.

Like many students pursuing a degree in Computer Science Engineering, I imagined myself in a bustling office, writing code in a cubicle, climbing the corporate ladder in a shiny tech company. It was the "expected path" — stable, logical, and neatly paved for someone who could speak in Computing languages as fluently as in their native language.

But even back then, something else was brewing. It started small — barely noticeable at first. Every exam season, classmates would gather around me not because I had the best grades, but because I could *explain* things. I had this knack for breaking down complex concepts, turning algorithm-heavy nightmares into something human and understandable. I would draw diagrams on our canteen benches, create silly mnemonics, or weave a narrative out of binary trees. They'd say, "Now it makes sense!" — and just like that, something lit up inside me.

I still remember one of my closest friends saying, "You should be the one teaching this subject, not attending the class." At the time, we all laughed it off — but I didn't forget it.

Choosing the Road Less Travelled

When graduation approached, the job offers came rolling in — at least for those who had mastered the script. Placement drives dominated campus conversations. Bulletin boards were flooded with interview dates, eligibility lists, and resume workshops. It seemed like everyone was running in the same direction, chasing the same goal: a high-paying job, preferably in a multinational company, preferably before the final semester ended.

At first, I tried to blend in. I attended the orientation talks, updated my resume, and even signed up for mock interviews. But the more I immersed myself in that environment, the more I felt like I was walking through someone else's dream. I couldn't feel the excitement my peers had. While they debated company packages and relocation benefits, I found myself zoning out, wondering why none of it sparked anything inside me.

By the time I reached my final year, I realized something had shifted. I had slowly — and silently — lost interest in the chase. The corporate ambition that once seemed like the natural end goal now felt like a uniform I didn't want to wear. I would sit in placement prep sessions, surrounded by classmates rehearsing answers about five-year plans and system design problems, and feel completely disconnected. It wasn't that I didn't understand the game; I just no longer wanted to play it.

I remember one moment vividly: we were in a packed seminar hall, attending a pre-placement talk from a well-known tech firm. The speaker was walking us through the company culture, career growth plans, and all the "perks" that came with joining them. Everyone around me was scribbling notes, their eyes lit with ambition. But I sat there frozen, staring at the slide on the projector that read: *"Your journey begins here."* And in my head, a voice whispered, *"Not mine."*

I quietly gathered my notebook, got up mid-session, and walked out.

Not in defiance. Not in drama. Just in peace. Because I knew, deep down, this wasn't it.

When I submitted my final term project a few weeks later — a project I had once thought would be a proud milestone — all I felt was a quiet certainty: *This isn't what I'm meant to do.* There was no excitement, no anticipation. Just a clear inner voice saying, *This path isn't yours.* I could tick the boxes companies were looking for — efficient coder, fast learner, team player — but the idea of joining a cubicle felt like squeezing into a space that no longer fit.

The idea of sitting behind a screen, debugging code for hours for someone else's company goals felt empty. The thought of measuring my worth through an annual package or appraisal left me cold. I didn't want to spend my life in meetings, worrying about KPIs or fighting for a promotion that would only bring temporary satisfaction. I didn't want to wait for weekends to feel alive. That kind of life — no matter how stable or prestigious — felt like a beautifully packaged compromise.

And yet, stepping away from it all was terrifying. The pressure to conform was enormous. This was the dream everyone around me had been preparing for, investing in, believing in. Walking away felt like rebellion — or worse, failure. There were moments of doubt: *What if I regret this? What if I'm throwing away everything I worked for?*

But beneath all that uncertainty was a quiet, unwavering voice: *There's something else you're meant to do. Something that feels more like you.*

That something had already started to bloom — in the way I helped my friends study, in the way I lit up when explaining concepts, in the fulfilment I found when others understood because of *me.* I hadn't named it yet, but the seed was there.

While others celebrated job offers, I stepped into the unknown — not with a contract in hand, but with a calling in my heart.

From Engineering to Education

Transitioning into education wasn't a clean leap; it was more like building a bridge one plank at a time, carefully and deliberately. At first, it seemed like I was stepping away from everything I had known: the rigid, structured world of engineering and technology. But in reality, I was just shifting the direction of my curiosity, focusing it on a new kind of problem-solving, one that involved human minds instead of machines.

The first step in this transformation came unexpectedly. It all started when, I met an educator at a family gathering — a casual party at my uncle's house. We struck up a conversation, and as we discussed my background in engineering, my passion for technology, and the shift I had been feeling toward something more meaningful, this educator seemed genuinely intrigued. I wasn't expecting anything more than a polite exchange of ideas, but to my surprise, the conversation quickly shifted to teaching.

By the end of our chat, this educator invited me to come in for an interview for a teaching position at their school. It was an unexpected opportunity — one I hadn't been actively seeking — but it sparked something within me. Without much hesitation, I decided to take the leap and explore the possibility. I hadn't planned on leaving my tech career just yet, but I was curious about what it would be like to step into the world of education. It wasn't something I had ever considered as a serious path before, but this invitation felt like a nudge from the universe. Maybe there was something to it.

So, I went for the interview, unsure of what to expect but eager to experience it for myself. The process of preparing for the interview was an eye-opening one. I was forced to think about teaching in a way I hadn't before — not just from a theoretical standpoint, but as a real, tangible profession where I could make a difference. It wasn't long before I fell in love with the idea of shaping young minds, of being the one who could open doors to understanding, spark curiosity, and help students find their own passions.

I spent my first days at the school getting a feel for the environment, learning what teaching actually looked like outside the pages of textbooks. I began to observe how educators connected with their students, how they inspired them to think critically, to challenge ideas, and to engage in active learning. I saw first-hand the impact that a passionate teacher could have on a student's life. It was nothing like the structured, technical world I had come from — but that's what made it exciting. The classroom was a place for growth, for exploration, and for constant innovation. I realized that teaching wasn't just about transferring knowledge; it was about empowering others to think for themselves, to solve problems, and to grow intellectually and emotionally.

As I spent more time teaching, I quickly realized that this wasn't just a stopgap, a temporary career change. It was a transformation. I had found my calling, a sense of purpose that had been missing in my life. The classroom became my canvas, and the lessons I created were my way of helping students unlock their full potential. I had never imagined that this would be the path I would take, but now that I was on it, I knew there was no going back.

To further immerse myself in the world of education, I decided to pursue a Diploma in Pre-Primary Education. At the time, it seemed like an odd choice for someone with a background in Computer Science Engineering, but it was exactly what I needed. I wanted to understand the very foundation of learning, how young children absorb information and make sense of the world around them. I didn't want to just teach; I wanted to *reach* — to connect with my students in a way that was meaningful, to understand how their minds developed, and how I could be part of that process.

The Diploma allowed me to explore educational theories, child development, and cognitive learning in ways that I had never done before. It deepened my understanding of the teaching process and how crucial it is to engage students on a personal level. It gave me the tools to create a learning environment where students were not just passive recipients of information, but active participants in their own education.

But even as I delved into the world of early childhood education, I knew my engineering background wasn't something I could easily set aside. It was part of who I was, and I wanted to integrate that into my teaching. That's when I decided to pursue a Bachelor of Education in Computer Science. This was the perfect way to combine my technical skills with my newfound passion for teaching.

The more I studied child development, cognitive theories, and digital learning tools, the more I realized how closely the worlds of education and engineering aligned. Both fields required an understanding of complex systems, problem-solving, and creativity. But teaching went beyond that — it also demanded empathy, adaptability, and the ability to connect with students on an emotional level.

I began to see technology not as something separate from education, but as a tool to enhance it. I wanted to integrate the logic and innovation of technology into the classroom, to create a learning environment where students could not only learn but also create, explore, and problem-solve. My engineering background provided a solid foundation for this, as I repurposed my technical knowledge to help students engage with the material in new and creative ways. Technology wasn't just for coding and algorithms; it could be used to enhance critical thinking, communication, and collaboration.

As I moved further into my teaching career, I realized that my engineering background had given me something unique — a way of thinking that was rooted in logic, analysis, and structure, but also open to creativity and exploration. I didn't want to be the kind of teacher who simply followed a set of instructions. I wanted to be the kind of teacher who inspired my students to think for themselves, to question, and to innovate. Teaching wasn't just a job for me; it was a passion, a purpose. And in that classroom, I found a deeper connection to myself, my work, and my students than I had ever found in any engineering role.

Teaching as a Choice, Not a Compromise

People often ask me — sometimes with curiosity, sometimes with confusion — "Why didn't you go into IT?"
They expect a story of rejection, disillusionment, or a career that didn't quite take off. But my answer is always the same, and perhaps a little surprising: *I did go into IT — just in a different form.*

You see, teaching is the most intricate, human-centered form of engineering I've ever encountered. In the tech world, you build software; in the classroom, you build minds. In IT, you debug lines of code. In education, you debug misconceptions, fears, and doubts. You optimize thought processes, create frameworks for understanding, and design systems not for machines — but for growing human beings. It's problem-solving at its most delicate and profound.

Every day, as a teacher, you test new strategies, gather feedback through your students' responses, and iterate to make your teaching better. You work within constraints — time, curriculum, attention spans — but the output is far more valuable than any product. Because when you succeed in this realm, you're not delivering a service or launching an app — you're shaping futures. You're influencing how a child sees the world, how they solve problems, and how they see themselves. What could be more meaningful?

Still, for many, teaching is often perceived as a fallback — a second-tier profession compared to the glitz of Silicon Valley or the security of a corporate job. I used to wonder why that stereotype exists. Is it because teaching lacks the glamour of the private sector? Is it because it's not packaged with perks and pay hikes? But I learned something through my own journey: the value of a profession cannot be measured in salary slips or LinkedIn titles. It is measured in the impact you create, and the legacy you leave behind.

I remember one moment that brought this truth home to me. It was during my second job interview, held in Ajman. I had already been teaching for some time by then, and this interview was for a more formal role at a reputed institution. Midway through the discussion, one of the interviewers leaned forward and asked, "Why did you choose teaching, especially with your engineering background?"

I paused. It was a question I had heard before — but this time, something deeper surfaced. Almost instinctively, I replied with words I hadn't prepared:

"Because it's in my blood."

That moment surprised even me. I realized as I spoke that teaching wasn't just a decision — it was an inheritance. My father and grandfather had both been educators. I had grown up hearing their stories, watching their dedication, observing how their students would greet them with respect long after graduation. Somewhere in the back of my mind, I had always associated teaching with honor, impact, and quiet strength. But I had never put it into words — until that interview.

It was as if my journey had come full circle. I hadn't planned to follow in their footsteps, but somewhere along the line, I had been pulled toward the very path they had walked. Maybe it was destiny. Maybe it was genetics. Maybe it was simply the cumulative effect of years of watching the ripple effect of a good teacher's influence. But in that interview room in Ajman, I felt a kind of peace, a clarity I had been searching for. I wasn't in teaching by accident. I was here by calling.

This realization changed everything. It reframed my entire journey — from late-night tutoring sessions to teacher training, from coding in labs to creating classroom strategies. I wasn't someone who had "settled" for teaching. I had discovered it. Unearthed it. Like a treasure buried just beneath the surface of my engineering identity, waiting for me to dig deeper.

Teaching was never Plan B.
It was always Plan A — I just hadn't decoded it yet.

If Chapter 1 was about choosing a different road, Chapter 2 is about discovering what it meant to walk that road — to build my toolkit, to connect with young minds, and to slowly shape the kind of educator I wanted to become.

I was no longer an engineer who taught. I was a teacher who engineered understanding.

This chapter wasn't marked by a single moment, but by a thousand small sparks — the seeds of curiosity that would grow into the foundation of my lifelong journey in education.

CHAPTER TWO

FINDING THE SPARK IN SCREENS

"Sometimes all it takes is one screen, one spark, and one curious teacher to start a quiet revolution."

Finding the Spark in Screens – First steps into EdTech

When I first began teaching in Bangalore, I was filled with a complex mix of emotions—excitement, curiosity, apprehension, and a quiet hope that I was walking the right path. This was not just a job for me; it was the beginning of an unexpected journey, one that I had never planned for during my engineering days. My decision to step into education was bold and somewhat unorthodox, especially coming from a background where the norm was to pursue high-paying corporate jobs in multinational companies. Most of my peers were busy cracking coding interviews and polishing their LinkedIn profiles. I, on the other hand, was standing at the doorway of a classroom—uncertain of the road ahead, but certain of the feeling that this was where I needed to be.

The school I joined was modest in both size and resources. It wasn't one of those elite institutions with sprawling campuses, high-end infrastructure, or international affiliations. It was a place that stood by traditional values, where discipline, sincerity, and moral development were held in equal regard with academic performance. The walls were plain, the furniture simple, and the teaching methods rooted in time-honored practices. There were no smartboards mounted on the walls, no digital displays buzzing with multimedia content, and certainly no tablets or laptops for students. Everything revolved around the blackboard and chalk—the classic tools of the trade.

Teaching here was about presence—about how well you could command attention, how clearly you could write on the board, and how effectively you could maintain classroom discipline without raising your voice. It was about storytelling, empathy, and repetition. Lesson plans were handwritten, worksheets were photocopied, and visual aids came in the form of handmade charts. Every concept had to be delivered through your voice and body language, with no screens to back you up or distract the students. I had to rely on the fundamentals: creativity, communication, and connection.

At that time, I didn't miss technology—because I hadn't yet experienced what it could do in a classroom. I was so deeply immersed in learning the art of teaching that I didn't even think about digital tools or online resources. I was focused on understanding how to engage a class, how to simplify a textbook chapter, how to deal with behavioral challenges, and how to make each child feel seen and heard. The transition from engineering to education had stripped me of the structured problem-solving I was used to, and thrown me into the dynamic, emotionally charged world of children's questions, laughter, confusion, and curiosity. It was unpredictable, challenging, and yet strangely energizing.

But even amid this analog world, a tiny spark began to flicker within me.

There were moments when I found myself thinking like an engineer again—not in terms of coding or circuits, but in terms of systems, logic, and optimization. For example, if a child didn't understand a math problem, I would mentally run through multiple ways of breaking it down, almost like debugging a piece of code. If a class was losing focus, I would analyze the timing, the delivery, and the pacing of my lesson—trying to "reprogram" the environment. And most of all, I was constantly reflecting: How can this be better? How can I do this differently? How can I reach more students, more effectively?

That curiosity stayed with me, even though I didn't yet have the tools to act on it. The environment may have been devoid of screens and gadgets, but the questions that lingered in my mind were unmistakably technological in nature. What if there was a way to visualize this concept better? What if I could show students how this works in real life? What if I could record this explanation so others could watch it later?

Of course, I didn't voice these questions out loud back then. There was no space for such ideas in that setup. The school was proud of its heritage and wary of too much change. But deep down, I was beginning to imagine a different kind of classroom—one where visuals complemented words, where interactivity replaced passivity, and where every student could engage at their own pace. A classroom where the teacher wasn't just a speaker, but a facilitator, a guide, and a bridge to knowledge that went beyond the textbook.

At the time, these were only thoughts—quiet, flickering ideas at the back of my mind. I didn't know that years later, they would take shape and define the very core of my professional identity. I didn't know that the seeds of EdTech had already been sown in that humble, chalk-dusted classroom in Bangalore. All I knew then was that something inside me had been stirred—and I was listening.

The True Spark

There's one story that always stays with me—a quiet but powerful moment that, in many ways, confirmed I was on the right path.

It happened during my early days in Ajman, shortly after I had joined a school where digital tools like projectors, smart TVs, and online platforms were slowly being introduced. While some teachers were excited by the shift, many were hesitant. For them, the digital world felt overwhelming and alien, like a foreign language they were expected to speak overnight.

One afternoon, a senior teacher approached me in the staff room. She was someone I deeply respected—graceful, wise, and beloved by students and colleagues alike. Her teaching experience spanned decades, and her classroom management was impeccable. But that day, her voice carried an unusual tone of vulnerability.

She looked around discreetly, lowered her voice, and said, "Can I ask you something? I've... never made a slide presentation. Could you show me how to start one?"

There was a flicker of embarrassment in her eyes—as if she feared being judged for not knowing something so basic in the digital age. But to me, it was one of the most courageous things I had seen: a veteran teacher, still willing to learn, still open to change.

I smiled and said, "Of course, I'd be happy to."

We found a quiet spot, and I walked her through the basics—opening PowerPoint, choosing a template, adding text and images, even inserting transitions. Her fingers moved hesitantly at first, pausing often as she looked at the keyboard. I didn't rush her. I explained patiently, step by step, and tailored the guidance to her pace. I could see the nervousness slowly give way to curiosity—and then joy. By the end of our session, she had created a complete presentation for her upcoming class on environmental science.

The next day, she used it.

She stood before her students, armed not with charts or flashcards, but with a glowing screen and a sense of pride. She navigated the slides with confidence, and the class responded with enthusiasm. The content hadn't changed—but the *experience* had. The visuals captivated the students, and the teacher, once wary of technology, beamed with energy.

Later that week, she came up to me, touched my arm gently, and said something I'll never forget:

"You made me feel young again."

In that moment, I felt the true power of EdTech.

It's easy to think of educational technology in terms of tools—smartboards, coding kits, interactive apps, robotics labs. But what truly matters isn't the hardware or software—it's the human experience it enhances. It's not about making classrooms look modern; it's about making educators feel capable, relevant, and inspired again.

That moment taught me something fundamental:

"Educational technology is not about replacing teachers. It's about empowering them."

It's about offering support, not scrutiny. It's about saying, "Here's something new—try it. You're not alone." When a teacher gains digital confidence, it ripples outward—impacting the quality of their teaching, their connection with students, and their own sense of purpose. And as a practitioner in this space, one of our core responsibilities is to be that support system—to offer encouragement, empathy, and hands-on help.

In many teacher training sessions I now lead, I share this story to make a point:

Never underestimate the courage it takes for an experienced educator to admit they don't know something. And never underestimate the impact of simply sitting beside them and saying,

"Let's do this together."

As schools continue to evolve, and classrooms become more connected, we must carry this mindset forward. For technology to truly transform education, it must first be rooted in trust, humility, and the belief that every educator—no matter their age or experience—can learn, adapt, and thrive.

This is where EdTech begins: not in the device, but in the decision to grow.

Building Bridges

My technical background gave me an advantage—but it was never just about knowing how to use tools. The real edge was empathy.

I had walked the same uncertain road many of my colleagues were on. I knew what it felt like to be thrown into unfamiliar systems, to hear words like *"Blooms Taxonamy," "Blended Learning," "Gamification,"* and feel completely lost. So when technology began entering the classrooms in Ajman, I didn't introduce myself as a tech-savvy expert or try to impress anyone with flashy tools. I came in as a *fellow teacher*—someone who understood the chalk-dusted corners of a blackboard classroom just as well as the glow of a smartboard screen.

And that made all the difference.

Instead of conducting top-down training or rattling off jargon, I started by simply sharing. "Here's something I tried with my class," I would say. Or, "This helped me make grading easier—want to give it a go?" Small, gentle steps. No pressure. No expectation. Just a willingness to walk with them, not ahead of them.

What many schools fail to understand is that the *resistance* to educational technology is often not due to unwillingness—it's due to fear. Fear of failure. Fear of being seen as incompetent. Fear of change that feels more like replacement than improvement.

So, I made it my mission to build bridges—not just between chalk and code, but between *comfort* and *curiosity*.

This meant redesigning staff sessions into interactive experiences instead of lectures. It meant giving teachers time to *play* with tools before being expected to *teach* with them. I introduced simple digital wins—interactive quizzes using platforms like Kahoot or Quizziz, screen recording apps to flip classrooms, or using Google Slides collaboratively in real-time. And every time a teacher's eyes lit up with understanding or excitement, a bridge was built.

The spark that started in those classrooms eventually grew into something much larger. With every small success, my own confidence deepened—and so did my hunger to learn more. I dove into digital learning platforms, experimented with formative assessment tools like Padlet and EdPuzzle, explored interactive storytelling through Scratch, and began integrating robotics and basic programming into my curriculum.

But here's what I always reminded myself—and what I share with every teacher I train today:

""Screens don't replace teachers—they amplify them.""

A smartboard can't feel the pulse of a classroom. An app can't adjust to a child's emotional state or recognize when to pause a lesson for a deeper discussion. But when used with purpose, technology enhances what great teachers already do best: connect, engage, and inspire.

A Stepping Stone, not a Shortcut: Embracing Change, One Click at a Time

That first experience with educational technology in Ajman wasn't a lightning bolt of expertise or a leap into cutting-edge innovation. I wasn't designing virtual classrooms or working with AI tutors. But what I *was* doing was something far more powerful: I was learning to be *curious again.*

In 2016, educational trends across the globe—and especially in forward-thinking schools in the UAE—were beginning to shift. The term *"digital classroom"* had started making its way into staff meetings. Interactive whiteboards were replacing chalkboards. Classrooms were experimenting with projectors, Smart TVs, and early learning management systems like Google Classroom and Edmodo. Teachers were starting to feel the pressure—not just to teach, but to *evolve*.

Yet not everyone was ready. Many were overwhelmed. Terms like *blended learning, flipped classrooms*, and *21ˢᵗ-century skills* sounded intimidating to those used to paper-based systems. In some schools, even turning on the projector came with its own learning curve. And here I was—new, relatively young, and with a background in engineering—seen as the one who could "figure things out."

So, no, Ajman wasn't just a job change. It was a transformation.

It was the place where my two worlds—**technology and teaching**—finally met and shook hands. It was where I realized that embracing change didn't mean abandoning the past. It meant *enhancing it*. It meant using the logic and problem-solving I had learned in engineering to bring creativity and clarity into the classroom.

A Practical Guide for Teachers: Starting Small, Growing Bold

If you are a teacher standing at the edge of this technological shift, unsure where to begin, here's what I learned—through trial, error, and plenty of humbling moments:

1. **Technology is Not a Shortcut to Better Teaching. It's a Stepping Stone to Deeper Learning.**

Don't use tech to rush through your lesson. Use it to *enrich* your lesson. An animation doesn't replace a well-told story—it enhances it. A quiz app doesn't replace formative assessment—it adds *immediacy* and *feedback*.

2. **In 2016, EdTech Was About Confidence, Not Complexity.**

The trend wasn't just about fancy tools—it was about empowering educators. Tools like Google Slides, Kahoot, and even simple screen sharing helped teachers bring lessons to life. Start with what's familiar and build slowly. Mastering the basics builds credibility and confidence.

3. Create a "Digital Warm-Up" for Yourself.

Before diving into full-blown tech integration, experiment with tools privately. Try creating your own lesson video. Make a quiz for your friends. Use apps like Canva or Prezi to make your first interactive slide. The less pressure you put on yourself in the beginning, the more likely you are to stick with it.

4. See Every Tool as a Bridge, Not a Replacement.

Technology doesn't replace your expertise. A pre-recorded video won't know your students' learning styles. A game won't pick up on emotional cues. But these tools *amplify* what you already do well—if used with intention.

5. Your Comfort Zone is the First Classroom You Must Outgrow.

I didn't walk into my classroom knowing how to use Smart TVs or interactive whiteboards. I had to explore. I had to make mistakes. But I made peace with being a learner, not just a teacher—and that changed everything.

Looking back, I now understand that my time in Ajman was never just about surviving a new teaching job. It was about *redefining what it means to teach*. It was about stepping into a new era of education—not with fear, but with wonder.

If there's one thing I would say to my younger self back in that first staff meeting in 2016, it's this:

You're not just learning technology. You're learning to lead change.

And it all begins—not with a shortcut—but with a small, intentional step.

CHAPTER THREE

CURIOSITY OVER CURRICULUM

"The best lessons don't start with a PowerPoint—they start with a question."

Curiosity Over Curriculum – Letting students lead with questions

Education, at its heart, is about curiosity. When I first started teaching, like many new educators, I clung tightly to my lesson plans. I thought structure equalled success. The textbook was my anchor, the curriculum my map. But soon, I noticed something: the more I lectured, the more eyes glazed over. But when I paused and asked a question—*a real one*—the room lit up. That moment was when I noticed a pattern: the most engaged, motivated students were always the ones asking questions. The students who had an innate desire to understand the world around them were the ones who excelled, not necessarily because they memorized everything perfectly, but because they approached learning as an ongoing process of exploration.

It taught me this simple truth: learning doesn't begin with teaching; it begins with wondering. And students, when given permission to wonder, are far more capable than we often realize.

The Curiosity-Driven Classroom

Why Curiosity? In traditional models of education, success is often defined by "covering" the syllabus. But in the process of covering everything, we often uncover nothing. Students memorize formulas, rehearse facts, and regurgitate definitions—but rarely *engage* with what they're learning. I remember particular moments in my teaching career when my students raised their hand in the middle of a lesson, their face alight with excitement. They asked:

"Miss, how does a robot 'see' with sensors?"
"Why can't we make our own games like the ones on the app store?"
"If the internet is in the cloud, can we ever really see it?"

These weren't in the textbook. But they became the gateway to deep learning. I realized that the best moments in my classroom came not when I delivered answers, but when students asked questions I couldn't immediately answer. It made me realize that curiosity is the greatest tool we have as educators. Rather than force-feed information into students, why not empower them to find the answers themselves?

This moment reinforced my belief that a successful classroom environment isn't about dictating content but about fostering the student's ability to lead their learning through questioning. The curiosity-driven approach allows students to explore, think critically, and problem-solve on their own.

Shifting the Role: From Teaching to Facilitating

When we think about traditional teaching methods, it's easy to imagine a teacher standing at the front of the classroom, delivering a lecture while students take notes. While that model certainly has its place, it often limits the potential for students to dive deeply into material in ways that truly engage their curiosity.

By adopting a more student-centered approach, I began to move away from being the sole source of information. Instead, I became more of a guide—offering resources, posing questions, and encouraging independent research. This shift required me to rethink my role—not as the source of all knowledge, but as the designer of learning experiences. I began crafting lessons that started with provocations or challenges instead of definitions. I brought in real-world problems. I left space for detours, rabbit holes, and what-ifs.

A robotics class that was supposed to teach motion sensors turned into a student-led investigation on how self-driving cars work.

A coding class about loops transformed into a game-building challenge inspired by what students were already playing at home.

It wasn't chaos. It was *controlled curiosity*—and it worked.

Tech Tips – Tools to Fuel Curiosity

As educators, our challenge is to cultivate that natural curiosity in a way that keeps pace with the rapidly evolving tech landscape. Whether you're teaching robotics, coding, science, or even language, the right tools can turn passive learners into passionate explorers.

Here is a selection of **innovative and practical tech tools** that educators can incorporate into their lessons to ignite wonder, foster critical thinking, and engage students in deeper learning experiences.

1. AI-Powered Inquiry with Curipod

Curipod is a tool that allows teachers and students to co-create lessons using AI-generated prompts. Its interactive interface encourages students to ask questions, spark discussions, and explore content beyond surface-level understanding.

Classroom Use:
Teachers can start a lesson with a thought-provoking question like, *"What if machines could feel emotions?"* Students then use Curipod to explore different perspectives, research, and even create their own slides with AI assistance. This shifts the classroom from content delivery to *content discovery*.

Impact on Curiosity:
It transforms students into active participants, giving them agency over their own learning journey.

2. Gamified Learning with Code Adventures

Gamified platforms like **Tynker**, **CodeMonkey**, or even **Replit's 100 Days of Code** turn abstract programming concepts into engaging game-like challenges.

Classroom Use:
Create small missions or competitions: "Who can solve today's bug fastest?" or "Design a game that teaches addition." These platforms reward experimentation and problem-solving, two skills closely tied to curiosity.

Impact on Curiosity:
Students learn to approach failure not with frustration, but fascination — gamification makes "debugging" a puzzle rather than a chore.

3. Collaborative Thinking Boards with Miro or FigJam

Digital whiteboards like **Miro** or **FigJam** support collaborative thinking, visual planning, and brainstorming in real-time — even in hybrid or online environments.

Classroom Use:
Start a session with a "Wonder Wall" — a board where students drop digital sticky notes about things they're curious about. Use it for group planning, visual coding (flowcharts), or even mapping out how a sensor-based robot might work.

Impact on Curiosity:
Students engage in "visible thinking," allowing them to connect and build on each other's ideas, fueling collective curiosity.

4. Augmented and Virtual Reality Learning
Tools like **CoSpaces Edu** and **Merge Cube** let students step into virtual environments or build their own AR experiences.

Classroom Use:
Students can simulate walking through a 3D model of a space station, explore the layers of a volcano, or design their own virtual museum about clean energy.

Impact on Curiosity:
This immersive approach bridges abstract content with lived experience, making even the most complex topics feel tangible and real.

5. Student Podcasts for Reflective Expression
Platforms like **Spotify for Podcasters** allow students to record and publish their own audio content.

Classroom Use:
Encourage students to host mini-podcasts where they explain STEM concepts, interview classmates about tech trends, or share reflections on recent robotics challenges.

Impact on Curiosity:
The act of preparing a podcast demands deeper understanding — and students love the idea of having their voice heard beyond the classroom.

6. Cyber Escape Rooms
Breakout-style learning tools like **Breakout EDU** or interactive platforms like **Genially** allow teachers to create digital escape room puzzles.

Classroom Use:
Design a cybersecurity-themed escape room where students must identify phishing attempts, unlock passwords, or detect a computer virus to escape.

Impact on Curiosity:
This turns learning into a challenge — a game of clues and critical

thinking that makes students *want* to know more.

7. Tech Journaling in the Real World

Students use tools like **Wakelet, Canva,** or even **Notion** to document and reflect on their interactions with everyday technology.

Classroom Use:

Ask students to capture how tech is used around them — the smart fridge at home, a traffic light sensor, a barcode scanner — and explain the science behind it.

Impact on Curiosity:

This cultivates awareness and appreciation of the invisible technologies shaping our world.

8. Mini Hackathons for Young Innovators

Using basic tools like **Google Slides, TinkerCAD,** and presentation apps, you can simulate a real-world hackathon experience.

Classroom Use:

Give students a real-world problem — like "Design a device that helps elderly people remember medications" — and let them ideate, prototype, and present in teams.

Impact on Curiosity:

Students learn design thinking and see themselves as inventors — not just learners.

9. Global Virtual Exchanges

Platforms like **Flip (by Microsoft)**or **Empatico** connect students from around the world in a safe environment.

Classroom Use:

Organize a coding or STEM challenge with a class from another country. Let students exchange short video diaries about their approach to solving the problem.

Impact on Curiosity:

Global collaboration broadens students' worldviews and encourages them to ask "How do other kids solve this?" — a powerful motivator for exploration.

Sample Lesson Plan: Question-First Robotics Lesson

Topic: Introduction to Motion Sensors
Grade Level: 6–8
Objective: Understand how ultrasonic sensors help robots detect obstacles.

Step-by-Step:

1. **Kick-off with a Question:**
   "How do robots know when to stop moving forward?"
2. **Watch & Wonder (5 min):**
   Show a short video of a self-driving car or vacuum robot avoiding walls.
3. **Mini Inquiry Groups (10 min):**
   Students brainstorm what kind of "eyes" a robot might have and write their ideas on sticky notes or a shared digital board.
4. **Hands-On Build (20 min):**
   Use Arduino or similar kits with ultrasonic sensors. Let students test distance detection.
5. **Share & Reflect (10 min):**
   Groups explain how the sensor worked and what real-world problems this could solve.
6. **Challenge Extension:**
   "Can you design a robot that stops *before* it hits something—like a cat in front of it?"

Student Project Brief

Project 1: "The Question Jar"

Project Name: Ask, Design, Build!
Duration: 2 Weeks
Goal: Let students choose a tech-related question and design a mini project to explore it.
Guidelines:

1. Pick a question you're genuinely curious about.
2. Research using safe, teacher-approved sites.
3. Use Scratch, Tinkercad, or any available tool to represent your idea (e.g., animation, game, prototype).
4. Present your question, your process, and what you learned.

Examples of Student Questions:

- "Can I build a game that teaches math to younger kids?"
- "What does AI really mean, and can I create a chatbot?"
- "How does an elevator know which floor to stop on?"

Project 2: "Building an Algorithm for a Virtual Pet"

Objective: To design an algorithm for a virtual pet game where the pet's behavior is determined by a set of user-inputted parameters.
Instructions:

1. **Create the Algorithm:** Design an algorithm that determines the pet's mood based on the time of day, how much it has been fed, and how much it has been played with.
2. **Develop the Program:** Using a programming language like Scratch or Python, write the code for the pet's behavior based

on your algorithm.

3. **Test and Refine**: Allow students to test the virtual pet with various inputs and observe its behavior. Encourage them to make adjustments based on the outcomes.

4. **Share and Discuss**: Have each student present their virtual pet and explain the algorithm they created. Discuss how changing certain inputs affects the pet's behavior.

Some of my most powerful teaching moments happened when I admitted, "I don't know. Let's find out together." It changed the dynamic. Students didn't just see me as a teacher; they saw me as a co-learner. That humility opened the door to exploration, failure, experimentation—and growth.

Curiosity-based learning doesn't mean abandoning the curriculum. It means using it as a launchpad, not a limit. One of the greatest gifts we can give our students is the ability to ask questions—not just in school, but in life. The simple act of encouraging students to ask questions and giving them the tools to find the answers is transformative. It shifts their perspective from "learning to pass a test" to "learning to understand." When students are free to ask questions, their intrinsic curiosity leads them to explore topics on their own, seeking knowledge outside the walls of the classroom.

Curiosity isn't something we "teach" — it's something we nurture. With the right tools, we don't just teach students how to *use* technology. We help them see technology as a tool for *discovery*, *creation*, and ultimately, *transformation*.

Try This Tomorrow:

Start your next lesson with these:

- "What do you wonder about ______?"
- "What problem could we solve with this concept?"
- "How would you teach this to someone younger than you?"

In the end, curiosity is contagious.

And in classrooms where students are encouraged to question more than memorize, you don't just teach content—you ignite minds.

CHAPTER FOUR

CODING THE CLASSROOM

"Coding isn't just for computers. It's for curious minds, brave thinkers, and creative problem-solvers—especially the ones in our classrooms."

Coding the Classroom – Logic, games, and computational thinking

A Pause that Shifted Everything

After very few fulfilling years in the classroom, I took a career break to embrace one of the most rewarding roles of my life—motherhood. It was a chapter filled with lullabies, midnight snuggles, and countless tiny milestones. Though I stepped away from the physical classroom, my curiosity never took a break. While my days were spent nurturing my children, my evenings often found me in front of a screen, staying connected to the world of education.

During this time, I made a conscious decision not to pause my professional growth. I enrolled in and successfully completed my Bachelor of Education in Computer Science, which deepened my understanding of pedagogy, curriculum planning, child psychology, and classroom management. It also gave me the framework to merge my engineering mindset with educational theory—a blend that would prove vital when I returned to teaching.

Even from the sidelines, I noticed that education was not what it had been just a few years earlier. The world of Computer Science in schools, in particular, was undergoing a quiet revolution.

The Curriculum: Then and Now

When I last taught before my break, around 2015–2016, the Computer Science curriculum in most Indian and international schools (especially at the primary level) was still quite traditional. It focused on:

- **Basic digital literacy**: turning computers on/off, understanding parts of a computer (monitor, CPU, mouse).
- **MS Paint**: Drawing, colouring, filling tools—used to teach mouse control and creativity.
- **MS Word**: Typing practice, formatting text, inserting images.
- **MS PowerPoint**: Creating simple presentations with transitions and animations.
- **Typing tutors**: Improving keyboard familiarity.
- **Internet basics**: Understanding browsers, search engines, and safety rules.

These were important skills, but they followed a largely mechanical pattern. The objective was to make students *users* of technology—not creators or thinkers. Creativity, logical reasoning, and problem-solving rarely entered the picture.

However, by the time I prepared to re-enter the classroom in **2019**, the educational tech landscape had shifted dramatically.

A new wave of curriculum had arrived—one focused on computational thinking, creativity, and innovation. Students were no longer just asked to open a document and type; they were being asked to create algorithms, build games, and solve real-world problems using technology.

Here's what changed:

Before (2016)	After (2019)
Typing practice and paint tools	Scratch & Scratch Jr. for visual programming
Basic Word and PowerPoint	Block-based coding & storytelling
Focus on software as tools	Focus on logic, sequence, loops, and conditionals
Teaching ICT as a subject	Integration of ICT across subjects (STEAM)
Internet safety as a one-time lesson	Digital citizenship as an ongoing theme
No exposure to AI, IoT, or robotics	Introductory lessons in AI, Machine Learning, and IoT in middle school

This wasn't just a curriculum update—it was a philosophical shift. The role of the Computer Science teacher had expanded from teaching tools to teaching *thinking*. We were no longer just showing children *how to use* technology—we were now guiding them to *create, innovate, and think critically* with it.

My Own Transformation

Adapting to this shift wasn't instant. Even though I had stayed in touch with trends and completed my B.Ed., I still had to immerse myself in tools I had never used before. I began exploring:

- Scratch and Blockly, where programming became storytelling.
- Arduino and micro:bit, opening a door to physical computing.
- Code.org, which gamified learning logic and flow control.

- Tinkercad and EdBlocks, which introduced circuits and electronics through drag-and-drop simplicity.

At first, I was overwhelmed. I had to update myself rapidly, diving deep into new platforms, experimenting with block-based coding, and understanding how logic could be taught to children as young as six. But with every video watched, every code block clicked, and every lightbulb moment in a student's eye, I knew I was exactly where I was meant to be.

With every challenge there was a new breakthrough. Every concept I mastered brought excitement to my lessons. And each time I guided a student through debugging their Scratch animation or building a smart traffic light model, I felt the same fire that had once pulled me away from the corporate world and into education.

Turning Play into Purpose: Unplugged Coding and the Joy of Logic

Children love games. And coding, at its essence, is nothing more than a game of logic—a delightful blend of sequencing, pattern recognition, prediction, and solving puzzles. Once I truly grasped that, a lightbulb went off in my mind. Why not meet students where their curiosity already lives? Why not turn the classroom into a space where abstract computational concepts could be disguised as play?

Not every child is immediately drawn to a screen full of symbols and syntax. In fact, some are intimidated by it. But every child understands the rules of a game. Every child enjoys solving mysteries or finding patterns. This realization became the basis of how I began introducing computational thinking—not with laptops and software, but with unplugged activities that brought logic into the physical world.

Algorithm Races: Turning Instructions into Interaction

One of my favorite activities was "Algorithm Races." The setup was simple but effective. I would divide the class into small groups and give them a seemingly easy challenge: write a set of step-by-step instructions for making a peanut butter sandwich (or any other relatable, real-world task).

At first, the room would buzz with excitement and confident chatter. "Take the bread," they'd say. "Spread the peanut butter. Close the sandwich." It seemed easy—until we started acting out their instructions literally. I became the robot following their algorithm. If they didn't specify "open the peanut butter jar," I'd just sit there, holding it. If they didn't say "use a knife," I'd use my fingers (to their horror and delight). Suddenly, they saw how missing a step or being vague could completely break the logic of the task.

This wasn't just a fun game—it was a brilliant metaphor for how computers interpret code: precisely, literally, and without context. The students learned that clear, logical sequencing is everything. It was the perfect introduction to algorithm design—without even using the word "code."

Pattern Blocks and Sequencing Cards: Loops without Screens

Another incredibly powerful tool was the use of manipulatives—especially pattern blocks, colored tiles, and sequencing cards. These seemingly simple objects opened up complex ideas like:

- Repetition (loops),
- Conditional reasoning ("if this, then that"),
- And event-driven logic.

One activity involved giving students a string of colored tiles or image cards (e.g., red-blue-blue-red-blue-blue). I would then ask:

- "What comes next?"
- "Can you describe the pattern?"
- "Can you write a rule for it?"

These moments planted the seeds for understanding loops and conditions in code. What's more, they engaged kinesthetic and visual learners who may struggle with text-based instruction.

As students mastered these offline logic games, I noticed a remarkable shift. They began to approach problems with structured thinking. They started asking:

- "What's the first step?"
- "What comes next?"
- "What if this doesn't work?"

In other words, they began thinking like programmers—even before they had written a single line of code.

Why Unplugged Activities Matter

In today's world, we often jump straight into technology. But these unplugged experiences are essential for a few key reasons:

- Not all students have consistent access to devices at home. Unplugged coding levels the playing field.
- Before children can grasp abstract logic, they often need to manipulate something physical and see it in action.
- These activities spark conversation, teamwork, and storytelling—essential soft skills for future-ready learners.
- By the time students sit at a computer, they already understand the logic behind what they're about to do.

Tech Tip-Tools to Bring Unplugged Coding to Life

You don't need a laptop to start teaching computational thinking. Sometimes, the most powerful tools are paper, puzzles, and a pinch of imagination. These resources helped me create screen-free lessons that spark joy, curiosity, and serious logic-building—all without the glare of a screen.

1. CS Unplugged — <u>csunplugged.org</u> (Hands-on learning meets computer science.)

This treasure trove of free, curriculum-aligned activities turns complex topics like binary numbers, encryption, and sorting algorithms into games and puzzles. I've used their "Marching Orders" and "Error Detection" lessons in both classrooms and teacher training sessions. What I love most? Every activity is paired with teacher notes, learning outcomes, and extension ideas.

- *Best for*: Ages 7–14
- *Perfect when*: Wi-Fi is down or devices are limited
- *Pro tip*: Turn their "Binary Bracelets" activity into a friendship coding circle!

2. Code.org's Unplugged Lessons — code.org/unplugged (Where creativity meets code.)

Code.org's unplugged curriculum is my go-to for entry-level logic games. Their storytelling-based lessons like "Graph Paper Programming" and "The Big Event" are wildly engaging and link perfectly with later Scratch activities. I often combine these with movement and drama, turning my classroom into a live-action game board!

- *Best for*: Ages 5–12
- *Classroom tip*: Laminate key instructions for reusability in small group rotations
- *Bonus*: Every lesson comes with easy-to-follow visuals—perfect for substitute teachers too.

3. Hello Ruby by Linda Liukas — helloruby.com (Because every coder deserves a good bedtime story.)

This beautifully illustrated storybook series follows a curious little girl, Ruby, who explores coding concepts through whimsical adventures. It's a gentle but brilliant introduction to ideas like sequences, loops, and even hardware vs. software. Kids don't realize they're learning algorithms—they just know they're going on an adventure.

- *Best for*: Ages 4–9
- *Use it when*: Introducing logic to visual/spatial or language-driven learners
- *Teacher tip*: Turn each chapter into a mini project or scavenger hunt.

4. Turing Tumble — turingtumble.com (The most fun you'll ever have teaching logic gates.)

Turing Tumble is a physical puzzle board where students use marbles and gears to build real working computers. It's part Rube Goldberg machine, part computer science lab. Watching students connect marbles to memory logic is like witnessing curiosity collide with engineering.

- *Best for*: Ages 10+
- *Perfect for*: STEM clubs, gifted programs, and hands-on explorations of logic
- *Challenge*: Use Turing Tumble to model a real-world process like a vending machine or elevator logic.

Sample Project Brief

Project 1: "Debug the Story" – An Unplugged Coding Activity
Grade Level: 3–5
Estimated Duration: 40–50 minutes

Skill Focus: Logical reasoning, sequence correction, and collaborative thinking

Objective: Students will analyze a narrative for logical flaws, then rewrite the story using accurate sequencing and conditional logic. This exercise introduces the idea of debugging as a critical part of both coding and life skills.

Materials Needed:

- Printed copies of a humorous, flawed short story (sample included below)
- Highlighters or colored pencils
- Correction sheet template (blank lined paper or a story map graphic organizer)
- Scratch or Scratch Jr. (for optional extension)

Sample Flawed Story Excerpt

"Emma got on the school bus in her pajamas. She waved goodbye to her dog, made her bed at school, and brushed her teeth after lunch. Then she had dinner in the classroom and walked home during math class."

Watch the students light up with giggles and curiosity!

Activity Breakdown

1. Warm-Up Discussion *(5–10 min)*
   Ask: *"What does it mean to debug something?"*
   Connect the concept to real-life errors (like pouring cereal before checking for milk). Relate it to fixing problems in code.
2. Story Read-Aloud *(5 min)*
   Read the story aloud dramatically. Ham it up—use voices, gasps, and giggles. Let students hear the errors in real time.
3. Partner Debugging Session *(10–15 min)*
   In pairs, students use highlighters to mark at least three logic errors. Encourage them to justify their choices: *"What's wrong here? What should have happened instead?"*

4. Rewrite the Story *(10 min)*
    Students rewrite the story with correct sequencing. Advanced students can add "if-then" branches (e.g., *"If she's not dressed, she can't leave the house."*)
5. Sharing & Reflection *(5–10 min)*
    Volunteers read their debugged versions aloud. Celebrate creative solutions. Discuss how logic helps in both stories and code.

Extension Idea: From Story to Scratch Animation
Let students animate their revised stories in Scratch!

*   Use simple sprites and backdrops.
*   Introduce basic commands like *"when flag clicked"*, *"say..."*, and *"wait..."* to simulate sequencing.
*   For an extra challenge: Create "before" and "after" versions to show debugging in action.

CHAPTER FIVE

The Language of Bots

"Robots aren't replacing teachers—they're becoming their co-pilots."

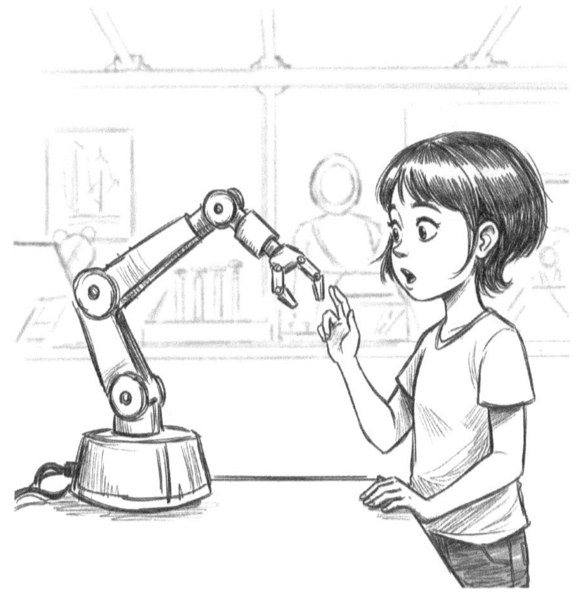

The Language of Bots – Teaching Robotics with Purpose

When we think of robotics in education, we often imagine sleek machines, futuristic labs, or expensive gadgets rolling across polished classroom floors. But the truth is, robotics as a subject has quietly been part of the curriculum for over a decade. It was there, tucked under broad banners like "Technology Integration" or "STEM Enrichment." Yet, it wasn't until after 2020—fueled by the global shift to digital learning—that robotics truly stepped into the spotlight.

The pandemic, paradoxically, acted as a catalyst. Schools scrambled to reimagine learning, educators began experimenting with new teaching tools, and suddenly, concepts like automation, programming, and engineering design became more relevant than ever.

My First Encounter with Robotics

By the time robotics became a buzzword, I had already laid the foundation. My transition from core Computer Science education to EdTech had opened doors. I was experimenting with block-based coding, integrating digital storytelling, and simplifying logic for primary students. So, when robotics kits started showing up in schools—Arduino boards, ultrasonic sensors, servo motors, and wheels—I was ready to guide both students and teachers.

I still remember the first project I supervised: a simple line-following robot. What fascinated me wasn't the bot itself, but the *process*—watching students troubleshoot a circuit connection, write their first if-else condition, and cheer when their code finally "worked." In that moment, the classroom transformed. It wasn't just about technology; it was about *ownership of learning*.

Why Robotics Matters

When people think about robotics, they often focus on the hardware—the wheels, sensors, wires, and controllers. But the magic of teaching robotics isn't in assembling the bot. It's in assembling *thinking*. Teaching robotics isn't about turning students into engineers overnight. It's about building *mindsets*—equipping children with the tools to approach the unknown with curiosity, confidence, and creativity.

Through robotics, my students have learned how to:

- Break down complex problems :
  I once gave my class a challenge: build a robot that could move in a square. Simple, right? Except it wasn't. First, we had to define what a "square" movement looked like, then break it into four straight paths and 90-degree turns. Suddenly, a small challenge became a lesson in geometry, logic, and sequencing. This process of simplification, of dissecting big problems into bite-sized tasks, is a skill they now use beyond the robotics lab—in writing essays, solving math equations, and even resolving conflicts.
- Think sequentially and logically :
  In robotics, if the sequence is wrong, the bot doesn't work. It's a powerful metaphor for life. I've watched students rearrange blocks of code 10 times to get it just right, developing a kind of grit and pattern-recognition skill that no worksheet could ever teach. They're learning to plan, predict outcomes, and revise—critical thinking in its purest form.
- Collaborate and communicate (Team-based learning):
  In one project, I asked students to create a traffic signal simulation. Some jumped to code, others to wiring, but soon they realized they had to talk—*really* talk—to coordinate their actions. They had to explain what their part of the system did, listen to teammates, and solve problems together. They weren't just learning robotics; they were learning *relationships*.
- Handle failure and persist :
  Robotics will fail. Sensors misfire, wires disconnect, batteries die mid-demo. But failure isn't the end—it's the beginning of learning. I've had students groan when their bot didn't move, only to beam minutes later when they discovered they forgot to upload the code. That journey—from frustration to triumph—instills a mindset of experimentation and endurance that I hope they carry for life.

In today's AI-powered world, these aren't just "nice to have" skills—they're *non-negotiable*. The ability to think computationally, work collaboratively, and persist through challenges will define success in the years ahead.

The Shift Post-2020

Before 2020, robotics was an optional extra—a "cool activity" that only some students in privileged environments got to explore. It was often reserved for after-school clubs, tech expos, or special STEM weeks. Many schools lacked the time, resources, or trained staff to include robotics in the core curriculum.

But when the pandemic struck and education was thrust into a digital frontier, everything changed.

Teachers were forced to explore new technologies overnight. Parents began sitting beside their children during online classes and witnessing first-hand what engaged or bored them. Administrators, faced with the task of making learning relevant, started asking: *How do we prepare children for a world that's changing this fast?*

And robotics answered.

Suddenly, robotics found its way into:

- *Computer Science Lab Sessions:* No longer limited to typing and MS Office basics, students began exploring programming logic and automation.
- *STEM Periods*: Robotics became the go-to hands-on learning module, blending science, technology, engineering, and math in one exciting package.
- *Design Thinking Modules*: From ideation to prototyping, students now used bots to solve real-world problems, nurturing creativity alongside critical thinking.

The change wasn't just institutional—it was cultural. Parents saw their children light up while building. Educators saw new paths to learning outcomes. And children? They didn't just learn—they *thrived*.

Teaching Robotics with Purpose: My Personal Approach

Teaching robotics isn't about tossing a kit on a table and saying, "Figure it out." It's about guiding students to find *meaning* in machines. Here's how I do it:

1. **Start with Stories, Not Schematics:** Robotics begins with *why*. Before I even mention motors or microcontrollers, I spark their imagination. "Imagine your grandmother finds it hard to remember her medication. Could we design something to help her?" "What if there were a robot that could clean classrooms after school hours?" "How could we help wildlife using simple technology?"

   These stories don't just add context—they create *purpose*. Students start seeing robots not as toys, but as *tools* for empathy. They stop asking "How do we build this?" and start asking "Who are we building this for?" That's when true learning begins.

2. **Demystify the Jargon:** Even words like "sensor," "loop," or "microcontroller" can feel intimidating. That's why I break it down like this:

   - A sensor is like your eyes or ears—it helps the robot "see" or "hear."
   - A motor is like muscles—it helps the robot move.
   - A microcontroller is the brain—it decides what to do based on the sensor's input.

   I create analogies, draw sketches, and even let them act like robots before we build. When students understand the *function* behind the form, the fear melts away—and curiosity kicks in.

3. **Integrate Across Subjects:** Why keep robotics in a silo? In my classes:

- A Mars Rover bot turned into a geography lesson on terrain types.
- A temperature-monitoring robot sparked a science unit on climate.
- A robot dog became the star of a creative writing piece—"A Day in the Life of Botty."

Robotics is *interdisciplinary by nature.* It blends logic, art, storytelling, math, and engineering. When we break the walls between subjects, students start to see the bigger picture—and that's where real innovation lives.

Tech Tips from My Robotics Classroom

Over time, I've experimented with shiny kits, confusing manuals, DIY hacks, and budget constraints. Here's what I've learned—the most effective tech isn't always the flashiest. It's what connects *with* your students, *for* your context.

1. Tinkercad Circuits – The Pre-Build Confidence Booster
When I first discovered Tinkercad, I felt like I'd unlocked a magic door. It became my go-to whenever I needed students to *visualize* what we were going to build—before touching a single wire.
We'd simulate blinking LEDs, motor speed, or ultrasonic sensors and even troubleshoot errors together. It was like building on training wheels, but with zero injuries and no burnt components!
Teacher Tip: Assign students a "virtual wiring challenge" before the actual hands-on build. You'll be amazed at how much smoother the real thing goes when they've done a dry run online.

2. Block-Based Coding: The Gateway Drug to Logic
My younger students were always nervous when they heard the word "coding"—until I showed them Scratch or mBlock. These

platforms made logic *visual*, playful, and forgiving.

I remember one Grade 3 student saying, "Coding is like making the computer play LEGO!" Exactly.

Teacher Tip: Start with a simple animation challenge—like making a sprite walk, blink, and say hello. Then relate it to robotics: "What if this was a real robot?"

3. Right Robot, Right Age

Not every robot is for every classroom. Trust me—I've made that mistake.

- For my early learners, Bee-Bots and Code-a-Pillar were perfect. Tactile, colorful, and no screens needed.
- For Grades 4–6, we used mBots and LEGO SPIKE—intuitive but expandable.
- For middle and high school, nothing beats Arduino. Yes, it has a steeper curve, but once they get it... there's no turning back.

What matters most: Pick a platform that makes *you* feel confident teaching it. Your comfort sets the tone.

Sample Projects & Lesson Ideas That Worked in My Classrooms

Here are some robotics activities that brought spark, challenge, and joy to my students. These aren't just builds—they're stories that gave purpose to code and circuits.

1. "Kindness Bot" (Grades 3–5)

Why we did it: I asked my students, "What if your robot could *help* someone today?" The result? A parade of helpful bots—one handed out kind notes, another reminded us to drink water.

Tools: LEGO SPIKE or mBot, block coding

Skills Covered: Movement, sound sensors, conditionals

Bonus: Some kids even made their bots dance when thanked!

2. "Debug the Library" (Grades 4–6)

Why we did it: We imagined a messy library with books all over the place. Students had to code a bot that followed lines to drop off books at the right genre zone.

Tools: Line-following sensors, mBot or simple cardboard paths

Skills: Line following, logic flow, loop creation

Outcome: One student named her bot "Dewey"—after the Dewey Decimal System. I still smile thinking about it.

3. "Mars Rover Mission" (Grades 6–8)

The hook: "NASA is hiring YOU to test their next Mars Rover design." Kids were instantly in.

Tools: Arduino/mBot with IR or ultrasonic sensors

Concepts: Obstacle avoidance, sequential logic, environmental design

Twist: Each team had to write a "mission log" from the bot's perspective!

4. "Disaster Response Bot" (Grades 7–10)

Context: After watching footage from an earthquake rescue effort, my students brainstormed how robots could help in real emergencies.

Build: A bot that navigated rough terrain (cardboard + pebbles!) and sent a blinking LED when it found a "survivor" (a heat or object sensor)

Lessons Learned: Engineering for empathy. We weren't just coding—we were imagining a better world.

5. "Eco Sorter" (Grades 5–8)

Inspiration: Our school's waste segregation system. Could a robot sort dry and wet waste?

Tools: IR sensors, servo motors, Arduino/mBlock

Skills: Sensor calibration, conditional programming

Extension: Students created posters to educate others on how the robot worked—and why it mattered.

No matter the age or tool, robotics works best when it's not just about code—but about *cause.* Ask your students often, *"What problem are we solving? Who are we helping?"* You'll find their logic gets sharper, but more importantly—their hearts grow bigger.

A Note to Educators

You don't need to be a robotics engineer to teach robotics. What you *do* need is curiosity, patience, and a willingness to learn alongside your students. In fact, the best moments often come when students troubleshoot *your* mistakes!

Robotics isn't just a subject—it's a mindset. It teaches us that failure isn't final, wires can be reconnected, and every problem has a solution if we keep iterating.

CHAPTER SIX

TEACHING TECH WITH A CONSCIENCE

"We do not inherit the earth from our ancestors, we borrow it from our children." – Native American Proverb

Circuits and Sustainability – Teaching Tech with a Conscience

A Personal Awakening

My journey into sustainability education didn't begin in a classroom. It began at home, during a weekend cleanup with my children. As we sorted out plastic wrappers, discarded batteries, and broken toys, my daughter innocently asked, "Why do we throw away so much?" I had no answer that felt good enough. That night, I realized that if I couldn't explain it simply, I wasn't just failing as a parent—I was missing a vital opportunity as a teacher.

That moment shaped how I would approach sustainability and the environment in my teaching. It wasn't about just recycling posters or one-time "green" projects. It had to be deeper—rooted in the real-world goals set out by the United Nations: the Sustainable Development Goals (SDGs). These 17 interconnected goals became my roadmap for bringing responsible citizenship, global awareness, and eco-consciousness into every digital lesson I taught.

Teaching in Qatar gave me a unique window into a country that has committed itself to sustainability from the highest levels. The Qatar National Vision 2030 prioritizes environmental development as one of its four pillars—alongside economic, human, and social development.

Qatar's Ministry of Education didn't just make this a policy. They translated it into curriculum goals, teacher training, and national STEM initiatives. Many schools introduced Eco Clubs, SDG-aligned science projects, and green innovation challenges that pushed students to think globally while acting locally.

Similarly, the UAE Vision 2031 positions the country as a global sustainability leader, aligning closely with the SDGs. Education in the UAE is deeply rooted in environmental responsibility, innovation, and global citizenship.The UAE Ministry of Education ensures that climate literacy and SDG education are part of every school's mission.

Sustainability education is no longer a "nice to have"—it's a must. Integrating SDG goals doesn't mean shifting entirely to environmental science. It means embedding values of care, conservation, and responsibility into existing lessons.

Teaching Sustainability Through Tech: My Experience

As an ICT and Robotics educator, I've always believed that technology should never be taught in isolation. It's not just about coding syntax or sensor calibration—it's about what we do *with* those skills. It's about making students feel like they can change the world, not just pass a test. That belief found its strongest expression when I started integrating sustainability into my tech curriculum.

It didn't happen overnight. It began as a quiet realization—an inner question I kept coming back to: *"How can we best integrate SDG goals in the classrooms"* I started testing the waters with small changes in my classroom, and what followed was transformational—for my students and for me.

Coding with a Cause

One of the first changes I made was reframing the way I introduced coding. Rather than starting with generic animation projects, I challenged students to create interactive stories about climate change. We'd begin with a class discussion: "What scares you the most about global warming?" or "What kind of future would you want to code into existence?"

Students took those questions seriously.

In Scratch, they built scenes showing the polar ice caps melting, the Amazon forest shrinking, or animals searching for clean water. Others created "choose-your-own-adventure" games where players had to make sustainable choices—bike or drive, recycle or toss, unplug or waste. Through these projects, abstract concepts like carbon footprints and deforestation became personal.

The most powerful part? When students began asking their own questions:

"Can I add a reusable water bottle sprite?"

"Can my game end with the planet getting greener if the player makes good choices?"

That's when I knew it was working.

Robotics that Responds to the Environment

With robotics, the possibilities expanded even further. I introduced a project called "Smart Green Tech"—a series of challenges where students had to build simple systems that mirrored real-world environmental solutions.

One group built an automated irrigation system using Arduino, soil moisture sensors, and water pumps. It detected when the soil was dry and watered the plants accordingly. The students didn't just stop at the code—they presented how this system could help farmers in drought-prone areas conserve water. They even calculated potential water savings per month.

Another team created a prototype of a waste-sorting bot, using LEGO EV3 kits and color sensors to detect recyclable items. They tested it with real-life wrappers and packaging, fine-tuning the code until the robot could confidently "choose" the right bin.

A student once came up to me during this project and said,
"I never thought my robot could help the planet. I thought it was just for fun."
And I told her, *"Fun is just the beginning. Impact is the goal."*

Digital Media with Purpose

Technology isn't only about code and circuits—it's also a language. A language through which students can express their ideas, hopes, and activism. I encouraged students to explore digital media tools like *Canva, Adobe Express, and Animoto* to design posters, infographics, and videos around sustainability.

They made awareness campaigns on plastic pollution, power conservation, food waste, and clean energy. One memorable project was a "Plastic-Free Pledge" video, where students filmed themselves making promises—"I will carry a cloth bag," "I will reuse my water bottle," "I will say no to straws." The video was shared on the school's social media and reached hundreds of parents and peers.

Some students even started eco-blogs and ran their own school-wide digital challenges, like "Green Week," where everyone had to share one tech-based idea to help the environment.

The real shift happened when they started seeing *themselves* as creators of change. They weren't just making things—they were making a difference.

The Takeaway: Turning Code into Care

These experiences proved something profound: when we give students real-world problems to solve with their digital skills, we teach them that technology is not the end—it's the means. And when that "means" is tied to sustainability and care for the planet, we don't just create good coders—we grow responsible humans.

Students began seeing their learning differently. A loop wasn't just a logic function—it was how we repeat bad habits that hurt the planet, or good ones that heal it. A conditional statement became a reflection of real-life choices: *"If I turn off the lights, then I save energy."*

Suddenly, algorithms weren't just instructions for machines—they were pathways to impact.

And the most beautiful part? It all came from their own curiosity, their sense of fairness, and their instinct to protect the world they live in. Technology simply gave them a louder voice.

Tech Tips: How to Make SDGs Part of Your Digital Curriculum

- Use Real-Time Data: Introduce tools like Earth.org, Climate.gov, or SDG Tracker to help students explore live data on air quality, water scarcity, or biodiversity.

- Virtual Field Trips: Use platforms like Google Earth or National Geographic's Explorer Classroom to "visit" deforested Amazon regions or Arctic ice caps.
- AI for Environment: Introduce students to beginner-friendly AI tools like Teachable Machine by Google to create models that sort waste or recognize endangered animals.
- Gamify Goals: Use Minecraft Education Edition's "Sustainable City" module or "Code.org' Climate Change" puzzles to teach serious concepts in a fun way.
- Digital Storytelling with Purpose: Encourage students to create videos, podcasts, or blogs raising awareness about an SDG of their choice. Use Adobe Spark or Anchor.fm for student-friendly creation.

Sample Project Idea

Title: "The ReBot – Waste Sorting Robot"

SDG Link: Goal 12: Responsible Consumption and Production *Ensure sustainable consumption and production patterns through innovation and waste reduction.*

Project Overview: In this interdisciplinary project, students will design, build, and program a functional robot capable of identifying and sorting waste into categories—plastic, paper, and metal. The goal is to help students understand the importance of waste segregation and how technology can support responsible consumption. Using kits like LEGO Mindstorms, Arduino, or micro:bit, students will apply logic, sensors, and creativity to automate the sorting process—similar to how modern recycling plants function.

Learning Objectives: By the end of this project, students will-

- Understand different types of waste materials and their environmental impact.

- Explore the principles of automation, sensor technology, and basic machine learning (optional).
- Learn input-processing-output flow in robotics.
- Apply conditional logic and loop structures to create decision-making algorithms.
- Develop presentation, collaboration, and communication skills.
- Reflect on the importance of sustainability in everyday life.

Materials Needed:
Hardware Options (choose based on age group and availability):

- LEGO Mindstorms / SPIKE Prime / EV3 kits (with color sensors)
- OR Arduino kits with:

  - IR/ultrasonic sensors
  - Servo motors
  - Load cells (for weight-based sorting, optional)

- OR micro:bit with attached sensors

Additional:

- 3 mini waste bins or labeled boxes (Paper, Plastic, Metal)
- Samples of clean recyclable waste or models
- Poster-making tools (Canva, chart paper, digital tools)
- Laptops or tablets for coding and presentation

Phases of the Project:
Phase 1: Explore and Understand

- Begin with a class discussion or presentation on waste types, landfills, and the role of recycling in sustainability.
- Watch short videos about recycling plants and smart waste management.

- Students research what materials are commonly recycled and what challenges exist in separating them.

Phase 2: Design Thinking

- Students form teams and brainstorm their robot concept.
- Use the Empathy-Define-Ideate-Prototype-Test model.

  - Empathize: Why do people avoid separating waste?
  - Define: What features would make a robot useful and easy to implement in schools or homes?
  - Ideate: What kind of sensors and mechanics would help?
  - Sketch a design on paper or use Tinkercad/SketchUp.

Phase 3: Build & Program

- Students begin constructing their ReBot using available kits.
- Basic Programming Logic:

  - Use color sensors to detect waste (e.g., blue = paper, yellow = plastic, silver = metal).
  - Use IR sensors or weight sensors to add another dimension of identification.
  - Servo motors or conveyor belt mechanisms for sorting.

- Test and iterate the robot's movements and logic.

Phase 4: Document and Present

- Students create a slide presentation:

  - Introduce their robot
  - Explain how it works
  - Describe the impact of proper waste segregation

- Design a poster campaign (handmade or digital) to promote waste sorting in school and at home.

Extension Ideas:

- Add a buzzer or LED light system to alert when bins are full.
- Collect real recyclable waste around school and conduct a ReBot trial.
- Include data logging—track how much of each material was sorted over time.
- Integrate AI or image recognition (for advanced learners) using Raspberry Pi or Edge AI kits.
- Invite the local waste management team to give feedback on student ideas!

Personal Reflection

I still remember the spark in my students' eyes when their robot dropped the first plastic wrapper into the correct bin. It wasn't just about sensors or servos—it was about realizing they had just automated a real-world solution. That's the magic of this project: it makes sustainability *tangible*. Every sorted item, every debugged error, every adjusted code made them feel like inventors—of a cleaner, more thoughtful world.

This isn't just robotics. It's responsibility, wrapped in innovation.

Real Stories, Real Impact

A few students created a water-wastage alert system using a basic moisture sensor and a buzzer. They tested it in his home bathroom and showed how much water was wasted when taps were left running. The project earned recognition at a local STEM fair—but more importantly, his family started turning off taps more diligently.

Another student group designed a virtual garden on Tinkercad to visualize how urban farming could work on apartment balconies. They even interviewed their grandparents about traditional

farming techniques and integrated cultural wisdom into the design.
These weren't just class projects. They were *life projects*.

A Greener Mindset, Not Just a Greener Lesson

We can no longer afford to teach students skills divorced from the planet they live on. As educators, we hold the pen that writes the next chapter of Earth's story.Whether you're teaching in Qatar, the UAE, or anywhere in the world, the message is clear: Our students must be equipped not just with skills, but with conscience. The future they inherit depends on what we teach them today.

By infusing sustainability through SDGs into our daily teaching—whether through code, robotics, digital art, or storytelling—we teach students the most important lesson of all: that their actions, ideas, and innovations matter.

And that maybe, just maybe, the future can be rewritten—one thoughtful, tech-powered solution at a time.

CHAPTER SEVEN

DRONE LABS AND STEM DREAMS

"In every young mind lies a sky waiting to be explored—drones are just the beginning."

Drone Labs and STEM Dreams – Making technology take flight

Recalling the moment that changed the way I looked at the sky—not through a telescope, but through the whirring blades of a drone.

It began with an unexpected phone call from my cousin, who works for a drone tech company in the Bangalore,India. "We're hosting a three-day event in collaboration with an IB school," he said. "It's about introducing kids to drone programming and flight control. You should come."

At first, I was hesitant. Drones? In schools? It felt a bit too futuristic. But curiosity (and cousinly persuasion) got the better of me. I went. And what I saw in those three days redefined how I saw STEM education.

The event was nothing short of magical. Children—some barely twelve—were programming flight paths, adjusting yaw and pitch like mini aerospace engineers. They weren't just playing; they were designing missions. Some flew drones through obstacle courses; others coded them to deliver payloads or simulate rescue operations. The sky had become their lab, and the thrill of flight had given new wings to their learning.

That event lit a spark in me.

Bringing It Back to My Classroom

When I first started dreaming of flight in the classroom, I wasn't thinking of expensive drones or high-tech labs.

It was the paper planes thrown during recess and students shouting, "Miss, look how far mine flew!" That natural curiosity—why some planes soar while others nosedive—became the perfect takeoff point for designing a flight curriculum that spans age groups, budgets, and disciplines.

The good news? You don't need to start with DJI drones or complex hardware. You can start with something as light as imagination—and a box of balsa wood planes.

Balsa wood gliders are more than nostalgic toys. They're tools of wonder. They cost just a few dirhams each, are easy to assemble, and—most importantly—they bring science, math, history, and creativity into one beautifully aerodynamic package.

We can introduced them during a "Wings of Wonder" week for the younger students. We can explore how birds fly, watched slow-motion videos of gliders, and then build our own.

Designing a Classroom Where Every Age Can Soar

When I began shaping my drone and glider curriculum, I asked myself one simple question:
"What would I have loved to learn as a child if I were handed wings?"

That question guided every lesson, every experiment, and every joyful classroom moment that followed. Because when we teach flight, we're not just teaching physics—we're igniting ambition, building resilience, and creating thinkers who look up and imagine what if...

Let me walk you through how this vision unfolded across different age groups in my classrooms.

Ages 5–8: Playful Pilots (Grades KG–2)

Focus: Exploration, Observation, and Storytelling

At this age, children don't just learn—they experience. They need to touch, move, and feel learning with their whole bodies.

In the classroom, we began with the simplest of wonders: the paper plane. It wasn't just a folded sheet; it was a character in a story. One student named her plane "Sky Sparkle" and imagined it rescuing birds caught in a storm. Another drew stars on the wings and said, "Miss, it goes to space at night."

We then moved to balsa wood gliders, gently guiding tiny hands through assembling wings and slots. With each piece they connected, I saw their confidence grow.

Activities:

• Building paper and balsa wood gliders using templates

- Learning the four forces of flight (lift, thrust, drag, gravity) through movement games (e.g., arms out = wings, jumping = thrust!)
- Story-based missions: "Fly your glider over the mountains to deliver food to baby birds," "Rescue mission to the island school!"

Subjects Integrated:

- Science: Introduce simple concepts like lift and gravity through visuals, role play, and short animated clips
- English: Creative writing and oral storytelling ("What did your glider see?")
- Art: Decorate gliders, label parts (wing, tail, nose), and build hangars using recycled boxes

Ages 9–12: Young Engineers (Grades 3–6)
Focus: Inquiry, Experimentation, and Introduction to Coding
By this stage, curiosity has matured. Students want to test ideas, measure outcomes, and build better.

We moved from just flying gliders to modifying them. I taught them how to bend flaps to see how flight changed. Some added paperclips to the nose to test weight. Others adjusted wing angles. Our classroom turned into a mini wind tunnel of questions.

Then came our first programmable drone—Tello EDU. With wide eyes, students dragged coding blocks and watched their drone lift off like magic. Except it wasn't magic—it was logic. And they were the magicians.

Activities:

- Modify gliders: Add rudders, shift weight, and adjust symmetry
- Run wind resistance experiments: "Which glider goes farther with added paperclips?"
- Use Tello EDU for block-based programming: Create flight paths, flips, and hover routines

- Record flight results in "Pilot Logs"

Subjects Integrated:

- Math: Measure distances, angles, average flight times, and chart progress
- Science: Study Newton's Laws, air resistance, and wing dynamics
- ICT: Use drone programming apps, flight simulations, and basic code blocks

Tech Tip:
For teachers new to drones, use DroneBlocks or Tynker with Tello. No wires, no stress. Just code, fly, and learn.
Ages 13–16: Drone Designers (Grades 7–10)
Focus: Real-World Application, Advanced Coding, and Creative Problem-Solving
This is where the curriculum truly takes off.
Students are ready to think like engineers. They're eager to solve real problems, not just fly for fun. So I challenged them:
"Can you design a drone that delivers medicine to a remote village?"
With Scratch and DroneBlocks, they created loops, conditional paths, and mission logic. We explored parcel drop simulations, and even practiced "return to base" missions. One group took it further—they designed a glider with 3D printed parts using TinkerCAD, and tested wind tunnel speeds.
Activities:

- Build and code beginner drones (Tello EDU, Parrot Mambo)
- Simulate missions: forest surveys, wildlife photography, environmental monitoring
- Design and fabricate gliders using CAD or recycled materials
- Explore drone maps with Google Earth overlays

Subjects Integrated:

- Physics: Analyze force vectors, thrust-to-weight ratio, and lift equations
- Computer Science: Loops, functions, variables, and debugging
- Geography: Plan drone paths over mapped regions, weather analysis, terrain types

Project Idea:
Make it cross-disciplinary. For example, assign one group to design the drone, another to code the flight, another to market the project (creating posters, ads, etc.). Collaboration mimics real-world teamwork.

Ages 16+: Flight Innovators (Grades 11–12)

Focus: Research, Ethics, Innovation, and Industry Readiness

At this level, students aren't just users of technology—they're creators, thinkers, and ethical decision-makers. The questions they ask shift:

"What happens if a drone enters restricted airspace?"

"Can drones be used for conservation?"

"How do I code object recognition using AI?"

These learners are ready for Python, JavaScript, and deeper dives into UAV laws and ethics. I introduced topics like facial recognition, drone privacy debates, and even had students pitch their drone startup ideas.

Activities:

- Write drone flight scripts using Python SDKs (Tello, DJI)
- Explore AI: Object detection using OpenCV
- Research real drone laws in UAE, India, and global airspace regulations
- Pitch a drone business idea: problem-solving + entrepreneurship

Subjects Integrated:

- Ethics: Surveillance, data usage, and moral implications of drones

- Engineering: Sensor integration, weight distribution, battery optimization
- Business & Economics: Cost-benefit analysis, startup pitches, market research

One of the biggest wins of this curriculum was showing school leaders and parents that drone education isn't an "extra"—it's an integration. Here's how it blends seamlessly:

- Math: Calculate velocity, acceleration, altitude changes
- Science: Understand forces, battery chemistry, weather impact
- History: Explore the evolution of flight from Da Vinci to drones
- Geography: Plan flight paths using real-world coordinates
- Language Arts: Creative writing on "A Day in the Life of a Drone"
- Art & Design: Design logos, drone shells, wings, and packaging
- Civic Studies: Discuss drone ethics, surveillance, and privacy laws

During one session, a quiet 8-year-old who had struggled with confidence approached me and said,
"Ma'am, I want to be an airplane scientist. Not a pilot—one who makes the planes."

I smiled, heart full. That was the moment I knew—this curriculum wasn't just about drones or gliders. It was about possibilities. About showing kids that their hands could build, their minds could code, and their dreams could, quite literally, take flight.

Drones can crash. Code can fail. Wi-Fi can lag. But the learning? That soars.

If you're an educator reading this, I encourage you—don't wait for a perfect moment or the perfect gear. Start small. Start somewhere. Because in every classroom, there's a future pilot, programmer, innovator, or dreamer waiting for their first lift-off.

Let's give them wings.

CHAPTER EIGHT

GIRLS WHO BOT

"You can't be what you can't see. But when you do see it—you become unstoppable."
— Marian Wright Edelman

Girls Who Bot – Gender, equity, and breaking barriers in tech

I remember the first time I had an interaction with a 11 year old girl from the USA, She had was quite indifferent about her first demo class in robotics. When I asked her what she knows about coding and robots Her replies were: "I'm not a tech person.""It seems too complicated.""Is'nt it a boy's thingy?."

It wasn't just disinterest—it was disconnection.

That's when I realized: I couldn't just hand her the same tools and expect different results. I had to change the blueprint.

A Room of Their Own

It didn't happen in a single moment or through a grand initiative. It happened quietly—over conversations, little nudges, and the gentle planting of ideas.

I didn't start a girls-only robotics club. What I did instead was simpler—but, in hindsight, more powerful. I began talking to my students, especially the girls, not about code or robots, but about women in tech. About the first programmers like Ada Lovelace, about engineers who built spacecraft, about women today who lead AI research and build life-saving apps. Not in lectures—but in stories, anecdotes, and casual mentions during class.

At first, they listened politely—some with interest, others with uncertainty. But I noticed their posture change, their eyes linger longer on the screen, their hands inch toward the kits.

That's when I made my next move.

Instead of giving them abstract or technical challenges, I designed coding projects rooted in their world—things they could relate to, things that made them smile.

I remember giving them a project where they had to use block-based coding to animate a ballet performance. The sprites pirouetted and twirled in sync with music they chose themselves. Suddenly, the conversation changed from "I don't get this" to "Can I make her do a jump turn?" or "Can we add stage lights?"

Another group coded a virtual pet game—complete with feeding time, sleep routines, and mood changes. It wasn't about robotics yet—it was about building with intention. Creating something meaningful.

Slowly, confidence replaced hesitation.

They began experimenting, helping each other debug, even staying after class to fine-tune their work. When I introduced them to simple robots later on—Micro:bit-based bots or line-followers—they weren't intimidated. They were curious. Eager.

I saw something magical in that transition. These weren't just girls learning to code. They were beginning to believe they can.

When Tech Meets Purpose

One student, quiet and thoughtful, asked, "Can a robot understand feelings?"

That one question became the heartbeat of our first big project—Mood Bot.

We used Micro:bit and LED strips to create a simple robot that could reflect moods—blue for sad, yellow for calm, green for happy. With each wire connected, each "if-then" block arranged, their eyes lit up. Not because it worked, but because they made it work.

Later, a small group took on a problem they'd noticed in our school garden—trash piling up despite signs and reminders. They created EcoSweep, a basic bot that could move around and sweep light debris into a bin. It wasn't perfect, but it didn't have to be. What mattered was that they saw a problem, and they believed they could solve it.

Then came Fashion Code—a project born from a love of design and a spark of curiosity about wearables. We learnt about Adafruit boards and conductive thread to stitch circuits into bags and hoodies that blinked with custom light patterns. They squealed with delight when they saw how it worked and when the jackets lit up. "I didn't know coding could sparkle!" one girl said.

Changing the Narrative

Soon, the energy was different. The girls didn't wait at the sidelines anymore—they raced to the kits, debated ideas, even challenged each other.

One of my proudest moments was when a Grade 7 girl, once too shy to speak up, confidently pitched her team's CareBot to a panel of teachers. It was a prototype designed to remind the elderly to take medication using recorded voice prompts and a simple time-triggered alert system.

She spoke clearly, her voice steady:

"This could help my grandmother. That's why we built it."

The Ripple Effect

What started as a quiet club grew into a movement. Girls began signing up for interschool competitions, taking leadership roles in group projects, and even mentoring younger students.

One girl wrote a blog post about her journey from being afraid of wires to building her own app. Another designed a sticker that read:

"Build like a girl: smart, strong, unstoppable."

CHAPTER NINE

DIGITAL CITIZENSHIP AND ETHICAL CODING

"The future won't just be written in lines of code—but in the values we embed between them."
— Tech Ethicist's Maxim

Digital Citizenship and Ethical Coding – Teaching with Responsibility

In a classroom, lines of code are not just instructions for a computer—they are reflections of values. We should often tell our students that writing a for loop or designing a game isn't just about logic—it's about intention. It's about asking: *What am I building? Who is it for? Who might it harm, even unintentionally?* Because teaching technology without ethics is like giving someone a map without a compass. Yes, they might reach somewhere—but they might also get hopelessly lost.

One afternoon, after a coding session filled with giggles, a student excitedly posted a picture of our class project on social media. It was innocent—just a proud moment shared. But the photo showed more than the code. It showed classmates, full names on the whiteboard, even the school's location pinned on the map.

That moment was a ***digital wake-up call***.

Instead of reprimanding, I gathered the class around and we had an open, honest conversation. What do we reveal online? Who sees it? What if someone uses that information the wrong way?

That spontaneous moment turned into one of the most memorable discussions of the year—and it changed everything.

From that day forward, digital citizenship wasn't an extra lesson. It became a foundation.

A Month of Cyber Awareness: Making Safety a Habit

One of the most powerful initiatives we took was dedicating an entire month to Internet Safety Awareness. Here's what we did:

1. Cybersecurity Drills

Much like fire drills prepare us for emergencies, these drills prepped students for digital dangers:

- Phishing Simulation Games: Students learned to spot fake emails and websites.
- Strong Password Challenges: Each student created and tested passwords using password-strength meters.
- Digital Footprint Exploration: We Googled ourselves to learn what the internet remembers—and how to protect our identity.

2. Weekly Themes
Each week of the month had a focus:

- Week 1: Privacy Protection – Activities on data sharing, device settings, and parental controls.
- Week 2: Positive Online Behavior – Role-play on online bullying, comment ethics, and empathy online.
- Week 3: Fake News Fighters – Identifying misinformation, analyzing sources, and using fact-checking tools.
- Week 4: Ethical Tech Creators – Discussions around AI bias, algorithm fairness, and inclusive design.

3. The Digital Citizen's Oath
Every class—yes, every grade—stood proudly and took the Digital Citizenship Oath. It wasn't just ceremonial; it was a collective promise. Here's an excerpt of what we said:

> ""I pledge to be a respectful, responsible digital citizen.
> I will protect my privacy and respect others online.
> I will think before I click, post with purpose, and code with kindness.
> I will use technology to uplift, not divide.
> I will be a force of safety and ethics in our digital world.""

This ritual created a shared culture. Even weeks later, I'd hear students say things like, "Wait, that doesn't follow our oath!"—and it made my heart swell with pride.

Future-Ready Activities for Ethical Tech Education

In a world where children can now build apps before they've mastered cursive writing, we must shift our focus. We're no longer just preparing students for exams—we're preparing them to design the future. And that future needs coders who care, developers who deliberate, and innovators who include.

So, how do we embed ethics into everyday teaching without it becoming a lecture?

Here's a list of meaningful, narrative-rich, and scalable activities—not just tasks, but mindset-shapers that will continue building digitally conscious citizens. These have worked in my classroom, and they can evolve with yours.

1. **The Digital Dilemma Wall**

Approach:

Imagine a bulletin board that doesn't just show student work—it asks questions that make them pause. "Should an AI decide who gets hired?" "Is it okay to post someone's photo if they didn't say yes?" Each week, I pin a new "What Would You Do?" card. Sometimes, it's based on real news. Other times, it's fictional—but relatable.

Student Engagement:

Students write anonymous responses or act out solutions in morning meetings. This allows even the quietest ones to voice their values.

Why It Matters:

Critical thinking and digital empathy grow naturally when students engage in gray-area conversations.

2. **Code That Cares Projects**

Approach: Each term, students pick a cause they care about—mental health, animal rescue, inclusive games, accessibility tools—and build a tech solution. A team can create a quiz that helps identify signs of stress and give peer-approved wellness tips.

Example Projects:

- An app that teaches younger kids how to spot phishing
- A Scratch story on bullying prevention
- A website advocating for digital inclusion in rural communities

Why It Works: Students take ownership, applying coding skills toward something personal. The shift from "What can I make?" to "Who can I help?" is powerful.

3. The Ethical Coders' Oath Ceremony

Approach: We hold this like a graduation—but for intentions. After learning about data privacy, cyberbullying, and algorithm ethics, students write their own oaths. We read them aloud, decorate scrolls, and even seal them in envelopes to open next year.

Impact: It's symbolic, but that symbolism sticks. Students refer back to these when faced with real-life tech dilemmas.

4. Designing the Internet of Tomorrow

Approach: I ask: "If you could rebuild the internet, what would you keep? What would you remove? How would you make it fairer?" This sparks wild, thoughtful ideas.

Activity: Groups sketch or prototype a new digital platform: A social network with empathy meters. A shopping site that hides brand names to encourage choice by quality. A news app with built-in bias checkers.

Tools: Canva, Figma, TinkerCAD, whiteboards

Outcome: Students learn design justice—technology as a tool that can include or exclude, empower or exploit.

5. Phishing Detectives: Cyber Sleuth Challenge

Approach: I stage a mock cyber threat—a suspicious email or text message—and challenge students to analyze it like detectives.

Steps:

- Decode sender address
- Identify red flags in language
- Check links using dummy URLs
- Rewrite the message as if it were real and safe

Follow-up: Invite a cybersecurity expert (virtually or locally) to talk about their job. Let students ask questions, like "Can someone hack a drone?" Spoiler: yes, and it leads to another powerful ethics lesson.

6. Digital Well-being Journals

Approach: We start with a simple prompt: "How does being online make you feel?" What starts as casual journaling often reveals surprising depth—overwhelm, comparison, loneliness, or even inspiration.

Routine: Once a week, students write or draw their digital experiences. They can track screen time, reflect on an online conflict, or even set digital boundaries for the week.

Outcome: This builds digital mindfulness, a skill far more useful than memorizing HTML tags.

7. Tech Talks with Families

Approach: We can extend the classroom by inviting parents to discuss how they navigate technology. Paremt's can share their experiences on digital safety and discuss about the latest trends like "How AI has become a part of their Job?"

Activities:

- "Decode This App" night
- Parent-student debates: "Is social media helpful or harmful?"
- Shared "Digital Diet" plans for home

Why It Works: Students see tech from adult eyes. Families become allies, not barriers.

8. Ethics in Emerging Tech: Mini Research Projects

Approach: Older students can dive deep into topics like:

- Should self-driving cars make ethical decisions?
- Can AI be held accountable for bias?
- What are the dangers of deepfakes?
- Should we trust emotion-reading tech?

Deliverables: Infographics, short videos, classroom debates, or even mock UN panels where students represent different countries' stances on tech laws.

Skills Gained: Research, argumentation, global thinking, and policy literacy.

From Screen to Society

Our digital lives are not separate from our real lives—they are extensions of who we are. Teaching students to be ethical coders is about preparing them to be ethical humans. When they leave my classroom, they don't just leave with apps and algorithms—they leave with empathy, accountability, and a mission to do good in a tech-driven world.

As teachers, we won't always have all the answers. But if we can light the path with reflection, empathy, and awareness, our students will go on to build not just apps—but a kinder, fairer digital world. Because in the end, the question is not just what they will build, but who they will become while building it.

CHAPTER TEN

MINDSET OVER METHOD

"Failure is not the opposite of success—it's the soil from which success grows."

Mindset Over Method – Growth, Grit, and Lifelong Learning

When I first walked into my engineering classroom, I felt like a tourist in a foreign land. The blackboard was filled with cryptic diagrams and algorithms. JAVA syntax danced across the screen in patterns I couldn't decode. Everyone around me seemed to nod along, while I sat frozen, quietly overwhelmed.

You see, I hadn't come from a coding background. I didn't own a computer at the time. The world of compilers, loops, and data structures was alien to me. When they introduced pointers and stacks in JAVA, it might as well have been Greek. I remember clutching my notebook with desperation, trying to scribble every word the professor uttered—only to realize I understood none of it.

There were nights I questioned whether I belonged in a room full of future engineers. But what I lacked in knowledge, I made up for with grit.

I stayed back after class. I joined study groups. I borrowed books, watched online tutorials, and often learned concepts three times before they made sense. It was not easy, and it wasn't fast. But slowly, painfully, things started to click. I wasn't naturally gifted at coding—I grew into it.

I failed a few quizzes. I blanked out during my first viva. But slowly, I found the rhythm. Concepts began making sense. The code that once looked like a foreign script began feeling like a conversation.

That journey, of coming from nothing to building everything from scratch, shaped my teaching forever. It's why in my classroom today, I never praise only the "fast finishers." I celebrate resilience—that stubborn little spark that says, "I'll get there, even if not today."

And that growth mindset, that raw persistence, became the most valuable thing I brought into my classroom as a teacher.

The Classroom Culture of "Yet"

Now, when a student looks at a maze of code and says, "I can't do this," I smile and gently add one word: "yet."

"I can't debug this... yet."

"I don't understand how this works... yet."

We celebrate failure as a part of the learning process. We treat every mistake as a teacher. Whether it's syntax errors or missed logic, we don't hide from our struggles—we study them. Our class motto? "Try. Fail. Learn. Repeat."

""A smooth sea never made a skilled sailor." – Franklin D. Roosevelt"

Building a Resilient Learning Space

Grades are just numbers. Growth is the goal. And to nurture that, I crafted a learning environment where students weren't just allowed to fail—they were encouraged to.

1.Feedback Loops That Empower

We need to replace traditional corrections with reflection. Every coding assignment came with questions like:

"What was your first approach?"

"What's a mistake you're proud of?"

"If your code was a story, what chapter are you on?"

This changed everything. It turned mistakes into milestones.

2. Failure Boards

In one corner of the class we need a bulletin titled: "This Didn't Work... But Look What I Learned!"

Every week, students could pin up something that went wrong—a broken loop, a wrong output, a design that flopped. No shame. Only learning.

Some weeks, the board may be more crowded than the achievements wall. And we need to love that. Because nothing teaches better than a misstep we bravely analyze.

3. Coding Challenges with Lifelines

Inspired by quiz shows, we can problem-solving fun and collaborative:

- Call a Classmate: Ask for a teammate's idea.
- Use a Hint: Request a guided clue from the teacher.
- Debug Together: Sit for a one-on-one code review.

This removes the stigma of asking for help. It teaches students that no one gets there alone—not in tech, and not in life.

4. Growth Journals

Each student should have a dedicated journal—not to list perfect scores, but to track their thinking journey.

- "I kept getting a syntax error—I felt frustrated."
- "Today I solved it! It was just one misplaced colon."
- "Now I understand that even errors have stories."

These journals become sacred. Some artistic students could add comic strips and doodles, turning struggles into art.

Life Lessons Through Logic

Teaching code isn't just about algorithms—it's about attitude.

Debugging a program often feels like therapy. You comb through thoughts (or lines), spot inconsistencies, revisit your choices, and try again. You learn patience. You learn not to panic when things break. You learn that walking away and returning with calm often reveals what brute force couldn't.

This is why I believe the most important line of code is the one that wasn't working—because that's where the real learning lives.

I will always tell my students, "You don't have to be perfect. You just have to persist." And I back that up with my own story. Of a young woman in engineering college who was the last to finish, but the one who never quit.

Future-Ready Resilience

In a world that changes by the hour, skills will evolve, platforms will shift, and programming languages will come and go. But the one thing that will always matter? Mindset.

Our students don't just need to know how to code—they need to know how to learn. To fall, get up, and keep moving. To remain curious. To ask better questions. To never stop.

Because the real curriculum is not in the syllabus—it's in how we face the things we don't yet understand.

CHAPTER ELEVEN

FUTURE-READY TEACHING – AI, INNOVATION, AND WHAT COMES NEXT

"The best way to predict the future is to create it." – Alan Kay

From algorithms to ethics: Introducing AI to the next generation.

The first time I introduced my students to ChatGPT, their reactions were a mix of awe and suspicion. "So... it can write stories? Solve math? Code?" they asked, eyes wide and curious. But what followed wasn't a passive acceptance of what the tool could do—it was a flurry of questions: How does it know? Is it always right? Can it understand feelings?

That was the moment I knew—AI wasn't something to fear in the classroom. It was something to question, to explore, to challenge, and to partner with.

In my classroom, AI didn't replace thinking; it provoked it.

We ran small experiments. I'd ask ChatGPT and a student to write the same creative story, and then we'd compare the results. Whose had more emotion? Whose felt more authentic? Whose had better grammar? These weren't competitions—they were conversations about humanity, machine learning, and creative expression.

Soon, our discussions evolved. We began exploring how algorithms work, how machine learning relies on patterns and data, and how bias can creep into systems not because of evil intent, but because of incomplete or one-sided data. We watched videos on how facial recognition can fail darker skin tones. We read about AI hiring tools that favored certain resumes over others. We even debated the ethics of AI art and music, asking, "Can a machine ever truly create?"

These weren't just tech lessons—they were life lessons.

Learning to Teach What Doesn't Exist Yet

Future-ready teaching, I've come to realize, isn't about being ahead of the curve. It's about knowing how to walk with the curve—curious, open, and unafraid to say "I don't know... yet."

As teachers, we were trained to be answer-givers. But in this AI age, I've learned that our most powerful role is being question-askers. The ones who model wonder. Who say, "Let's find out together." The ones who make room for thinking to evolve.

Students should not be afraid to explore a new AI tool. They should be able test it, break it, even critique it. They should be able to write prompts, examine responses, and ask things like, "What did it miss?" or "Is it being fair?"

AI as a Teaching Assistant (Not a Teacher)

In the classroom, AI doesn't stand at the front—it sits beside us. It's like a helpful co-pilot, not the captain of the learning journey. I've used AI tools to generate differentiated subject problems, prompt creative writing with story starters, troubleshoot blocks of code, and even run simulations in science and create images .

But the golden rule remains: AI can suggest—but we decide. It can assist—but we think.

One of the most memorable examples came from my grade 5 robotics club. A bright 11-year-old, Aarav, was building a simple robot car that could stop when it detected an obstacle. We had just started learning Python, and he felt a little stuck.

So, he turned to ChatGPT and asked:
"Can you give me a Python code to stop a robot when something is in front of it?"

ChatGPT replied with a generic snippet—straightforward, correct, but bland.

Most would have copied and pasted it. But Aarav didn't stop there.

He looked at it, thought hard, and said,
"This won't work for my bot. My sensor gives distance in inches, not centimeters—and I want the robot to slow down first before stopping completely."

He adjusted the code, added a condition to reduce the speed gradually, and explained his changes to the class. Then he turned to me and said with a smile:
"I used AI to get started, but it couldn't have solved my problem—because my robot is unique."

That sentence stayed with me.

It reminded me that true innovation lies in how students build on the tools—not how much they rely on them. At age 10 or 11, they are already learning a critical 21st-century truth: tools can assist, but human thinking leads.

AI isn't the enemy of imagination—it's the amplifier of it. When we teach our students to use these tools responsibly, critically, and creatively, we're not just preparing them for jobs—we're preparing them for a world where adaptability and originality are priceless.

AI Literacy in Schools and the Frameworks Shaping the Next Generation

In a sunlit classroom in Bangalore, a curious 12-year-old girl uses an AI-powered visual tool to explore how climate change affects her local river. Across the Arabian Sea, in a school in Ajman, a student is debugging a chatbot that helps new students navigate campus life. And in Doha, a young coder proudly presents her AI model that predicts recycling habits in her neighborhood. These moments may seem scattered, but they are all signs of something bigger: AI literacy is no longer optional—it's the new language of empowerment.

Schools across India, UAE, and Qatar are waking up to this shift. It's not enough to teach students what AI is—they must understand how it works, where it can be applied, and most importantly, why it matters.

India's National Education Policy (NEP 2020) made space for AI in school curricula, encouraging problem-solving, design thinking, and ethical discussions starting as early as Grade 6. Some CBSE and ICSE schools are already rolling out AI modules under Atal Tinkering Labs (ATL) and tying it into STEM clubs and coding curriculums.

In the UAE, AI is no longer just a subject—it's a national strategy. With the country appointing the world's first Minister of AI, its Vision 2031 includes strong AI integration in education. Schools are introducing students to machine learning, data handling, and robotics—often in partnership with global tech platforms. AI literacy here is tied directly to future workforce readiness and entrepreneurship.

Qatar, through its National Vision 2030 and the Ministry of Education and Higher Education, is taking deliberate steps to integrate AI across disciplines. The Qatar Research, Development, and Innovation (QRDI) Strategy encourages early exposure to AI-driven solutions in environmental, healthcare, and logistics challenges. In some schools, AI is taught through real-world simulations—students use AI to monitor energy usage, automate greenhouse controls, and even create assistive tech for peers with disabilities.

The future of AI education in these countries needs a common language—a framework that doesn't just teach AI skills, but cultivates AI mindsets. Here's what that might look like:

- Explore: Let students play with AI tools early—image generators, chatbots, voice assistants—not to memorize terms, but to develop digital curiosity.
- Understand: Introduce concepts like machine learning, neural networks, and datasets using stories, games, and unplugged activities.
- Create: Encourage students to build their own tools—whether it's a simple AI-powered quiz app or an environmental data dashboard.
- Question: Embed ethical discussions into every lesson. Treat AI not just as a product to use, but as a responsibility to guide.
- Reflect: Let students document their learning, decisions, and missteps. In the age of AI, self-awareness is a superpower.

The Teacher in the Loop – Guiding AI with Purpose

As educators, we're not just teaching about AI—we're shaping how the next generation will think with it.

To do this well, we must first accept a powerful truth: we don't need to be AI experts to teach AI responsibly. What we do need is a mindset of lifelong learning, adaptability, and ethical anchoring.

So how can we, as teachers, improve the use of AI in our classrooms?

1. Start Where You Are

You don't need fancy labs or complex software. Begin with tools that are already accessible—like image generators, voice assistants, or learning platforms with built-in AI. Use them not just for convenience, but as conversation starters.

For instance, ask students:

- Why do you think the chatbot responded that way?
- What data might it be using?
- Can we trust it? Why or why not?

These questions turn passive tech use into active inquiry.

2. Make AI Visible and Explainable

AI shouldn't feel like magic. Use analogies and everyday examples to explain how it works. Compare a neural network to the brain's learning. Use paper-based simulations of machine learning (like sorting objects or drawing patterns). Let students see the logic behind the tool.

3. Model Ethical Curiosity

As educators, we model far more than we realize. If we ask thoughtful questions about bias, consent, and fairness, our students will too. Integrate "AI Ethics Corners" in your lesson plans—5-minute check-ins where students reflect on who might be impacted by the AI they create or use.

4. Blend AI into Every Subject

AI isn't a standalone topic—it's interdisciplinary. Bring it into language lessons (AI-generated poems vs human poems), history (how facial recognition impacts civil rights), science (predictive models in climate studies), and math (data bias in statistics).

When AI is contextualized, it's better understood—and better questioned.

5. Celebrate Critical Thinking Over Flashy Outputs

It's tempting to be impressed when students use AI to generate slick presentations or perfect code. But we should celebrate how they used it—did they understand it? Question it? Improve it? Reflect on it?

Give credit not just for the product, but for the process of thought behind it.

6. Create Safe Spaces for Experimentation

Let students fail with AI. Let them misuse a tool and then reflect on it. Let them redesign their AI project halfway through because they realized it wasn't inclusive. Mistakes in AI are not errors—they are invitations to understand.

7. Stay Curious, Stay Humble

The world of AI will keep evolving. New tools will emerge. Old ones will fade. The best thing we can do is stay curious. Join educator forums. Try new tools in small doses. Learn with your students, not just for them.

Ultimately, the goal isn't to raise a generation of AI engineers. It's to raise a generation of thinkers, dreamers, builders, and ethical decision-makers who can lead AI—not just be led by it.

We need AI-literate poets who write with empathy, doctors who understand algorithmic diagnostics, and farmers who can leverage climate data. This is the future. This is what our classrooms must nurture.

And for educators like us, the message is clear:

> *"Teach AI like you teach values—with care, curiosity, and context."*

Tech Tip for Teachers: Guiding AI Use Across Age Groups

Ages 5–8: "AI as a Curious Friend"

- Use voice-based AI (like reading assistants or image-based search) for storytelling or answering "wonder questions."
- Focus on curiosity over accuracy—teach students to ask thoughtful, kind, and curious questions.
- Reinforce that AI doesn't "know everything"—it's okay to double-check with a book or a teacher.

Ages 9–12: "AI as a Helper, Not the Hero"

- Introduce AI tools like ChatGPT or educational bots in structured activities—writing story starters, brainstorming project ideas, or generating sample code.
- Always ask students to modify or improve AI output: "Can you make it better?" or "What would you do differently?"
- Discuss responsible digital behavior and the importance of crediting sources (even AI tools).

Ages 13–18: "AI as a Research Partner"

- Encourage AI use for drafts, data analysis, coding, language support, etc.—but require reflections or annotations on how it was used.
- Teach students about algorithmic bias, misinformation, and intellectual honesty.
- Assign critical tasks like comparing AI responses to real-world facts or analyzing ethical dilemmas in AI usage.

Adult Learners & Educators: "AI as a Professional Co-Pilot"

- Use AI for brainstorming, lesson planning, content adaptation, and administrative support—but maintain your creative and instructional voice.
- Model transparency: let students know when you've used AI, and how you've added your own thinking.
- Continue learning: AI is evolving, and staying current helps you guide students with confidence.

Golden Rule at Every Age:

""If AI did the thinking, the student missed the learning."
Always make space for reflection, editing, and personalization."

In this emerging world, the best AI teacher is not the one who knows the most code, but the one who knows how to ask the right questions.

Because in the end, we are not just teaching machines to learn—we are teaching humans to think.

"Let us teach AI like we teach empathy.
Let us teach AI like we teach justice.
Let us teach AI like we teach life."

CHAPTER TWELVE

THE GLOBAL CLASSROOM

"We may not speak the same language, but we code the same curiosity."

The Global Classroom – Teaching Across Borders, Time Zones, and Cultures

It's just past 4:00 a.m. in Bangalore when I log into my virtual classroom. A quiet hum of the AC fills the room as my screen lights up with smiling faces—some just rubbing the sleep out of their eyes in New York, others still sipping hot chocolate in California. And just like that, the borders blur, the time zones sync, and the classroom expands beyond anything I ever imagined possible.

This—this—is the **Global Classroom**.

But it didn't begin here.There was a time when my classroom had four walls, a whiteboard, and a fixed timetable. Then came the shift—first slowly, then all at once—and suddenly, my classroom had no borders, no single language, no one time zone. It was a mosaic of cities and cultures, of yawning students in pajamas on one side of the world, and bright-eyed learners just home from school on the other.

From Bangalore to Ajman to Doha: My Journey to a Borderless Classroom

My teaching journey began in the lively, tech-saturated heart of Bangalore, where curiosity was always in abundance but resources were sometimes scarce.I learned how deeply culture and community shape the learning experience. My students came from diverse linguistic and cultural backgrounds, and every day was a blend of tradition and technology. We celebrated Kannada Rajyotsava and Science Day with equal excitement, and I often found myself learning just as much from my students as they did from me.

Then came Ajman, UAE—a coastal city full of contrasts. In my classroom, traditional values met cutting-edge tech. I encountered a new kind of diversity—one shaped by expat families, multilingual classrooms, and multicultural values. It was here that I realized the power of technology to bridge linguistic and academic gaps.

Doha was different again. A city with bold ambitions, where education is deeply linked to national pride and futuristic visions. There, my lessons took on a new rhythm. I worked closely with students whose families were part of Qatar's growing industries. They asked questions that felt big—about AI, sustainability, data privacy—and I knew I had to elevate my teaching.

Each city taught me something irreplaceable.

""In Bangalore, I learned to innovate with less.
In Ajman, I learned to teach with cultural empathy.
In Doha, I learned to teach with purpose.""

And now, from the quiet corner of my home , I teach students across the U.S., and all those experiences sit beside me as I greet each new learner.

Teaching Without Borders: The Magic of Multicultural Learning
Something magical happens when your class is made of learners from different time zones, accents, and worldviews. You start to teach beyond the subject.

In one session, a student in California programmed a game to help kids learn about recycling. A student from Doha added features to track plastic waste. Another from India suggested a scoring system based on the UN's SDGs. It wasn't just collaboration—it was global co-creation.

We have celebrated Eid and Diwali, Christmas, and Thanksgiving. Not through slideshows, but through code, creativity, and conversation. A Scratch project showing Eid moon animations, a Thanksgiving gratitude journal built in Google Sites, or a Christmas bot that played carols—all built by children who had never celebrated these holidays, but who understood the spirit through collaboration.We celebrated Diwali with digital rangoli designs.

What started as code evolved into connection.

Teaching across borders taught me to be more than a tech facilitator. I became a cultural bridge, a time-zone juggler, and sometimes, even a translator of perspectives.

- I learned to slow down for students whose first language wasn't English.
- I adapted my examples—from subway maps to sand dunes—depending on where my students lived.
- I stopped assuming a one-size-fits-all model for curiosity.

And they, in turn, taught me.

A 10-year-old from Texas showed me how to build storytelling games in Roblox. A student in New Jersey taught me how to add virtual coins to a Scratch project. Another in Oregon explained their family's Native American history during a digital heritage journal project.

A New Kind of Teacher

When people ask me now, "Where do you teach?" I smile and say, "Everywhere."

Because I no longer teach in just a classroom.
I teach in living rooms in Ohio, study corners in Doha, balconies in Sharjah, and bedrooms in Bangalore.

And the biggest lesson I've learned is this:

> *"The heart of education isn't limited by place. It is expanded by perspective.*
> *The more diverse our students, the richer our teaching becomes."*

Appendix A : Sample Curriculum Maps

AI & Robotics Curriculum Map (Ages 10–14)

Building Thinkers, Tinkerers & Ethical Innovators

Module	Title	Focus Areas	Sample Activities	Skills Developed
1	Introduction to Sensors & Actuators	Basic electronics, types of sensors (IR, ultrasonic), simple actuator movement	- Connect ultrasonic sensors to Arduino - Build a "Hand Sanitizer Dispenser" prototype - Use LEDs and buzzers as output devices	Circuit logic, hardware-software integration, hands-on troubleshooting
2	Python for Robotics	Programming logic, conditionals, loops, real-time input	- Write Python code for obstacle detection - Build a line-following bot using IR sensors - Test and debug logic errors	Problem-solving, debugging, sequencing, computational thinking
3	AI-Powered Projects	Machine learning basics, vision & voice AI	- Build a simple face detection model using OpenCV - Program a voice-controlled LED system using speech recognition - Discuss ethical concerns of surveillance	Intro to AI, speech & image processing, ethical design thinking

Project Showcase: At the end of Module 3, students present a "Robot for Good" prototype addressing an SDG (e.g., Waste Sorting Robot, AI Plant Monitor).

Digital Citizenship Month Plan

A Month to Rewire the Mind, Not Just the Machines

Week	Theme	Objectives	Activities	Outcome
Week 1	*Online Safety & Privacy Awareness*	Help students understand online threats and personal data protection	- Watch & reflect on animated short videos - Poster-making: "My Digital Footprint" - Class discussion: "What would you share with a stranger?"	Students identify safe vs unsafe sharing; define digital footprint
Week 2	*Ethical Use of Technology*	Promote awareness on tech misuse, deep fakes, AI bias, and respectful engagement	- Case study: Social media prank gone wrong - Role-play: "You're the AI Ethics Committee" - Journal prompt: "What if AI made a decision that hurt someone?"	Develop empathy and decision-making skills; understand bias in tech
Week 3	*Cybersecurity Drill Simulations*	Train students in basic response protocols for digital threats	- Simulated phishing email activity - Build-your-own strong password challenge - Role-play: "Cyber Cops & Hackers"	Students demonstrate basic cyber defense behaviors and alertness
Week 4	*Digital Oath Ceremony & Student Presentations*	Foster accountability and digital integrity through ritual and voice	- "I am a Responsible Digital Citizen" oath (each class signs it) - Group presentations on "My Tech Values" - Digital Citizenship Wall (sticky notes with tech promises)	Build lasting digital ethics culture; empower student ownership

Capstone Highlight: Create a class mural titled "The Internet Starts With ME" combining student illustrations, quotes, and personal pledges.

Appendix B

Project Title: Balcony Urban Farming – A Smart City Solution

Tools & Platform:

- Tinkercad (Use 3D Design workspace)
- Optionally: Tinkercad Circuits (to simulate sensors like soil moisture or temperature)

Design Elements to Include in Your Balcony Garden:

1. Base Platform:

- Create a balcony slab using a flat box (e.g., 80mm x 40mm x 5mm).
- Add railing bars on 3 sides using narrow tall rectangles (5mm x 2mm x 30mm).

 2. Vertical Farming Rack:

- Use a stack of small rectangular boxes for planters.
- Add spacing of 10–15mm between rows.
- Include 3 tiers to show maximized vertical space use.

 3. Smart Irrigation System:

- Add a water tank (cylinder) at the top.

- Use tubes (thin cylinders or scribble tool) leading to each planter.
- Place a servo motor box (custom object or box + gear) to simulate an auto-drip.

4. Sensor Placement (optional – for Tinkercad Circuits):

- Insert icons/blocks for:
- Soil Moisture Sensor (in planter)
- Temperature Sensor (on balcony wall)
- Light Sensor (top shelf)
- Connect to a Microcontroller (Arduino Uno)

5. Renewable Element:

- Add a solar panel (flat tilted box on a stand) to power smart features.

6. Compost Bin:

- Add a small cylinder or cube labeled as a compost bin.
- This promotes waste-to-resource thinking.

7. Furniture (Optional):

- Add a foldable chair and small table to represent human interaction with the garden.

8. Label Each Element:

- Use Tinkercad's "Text" tool to add labels: "Planter Box", "Water Tank", "Moisture Sensor", etc.

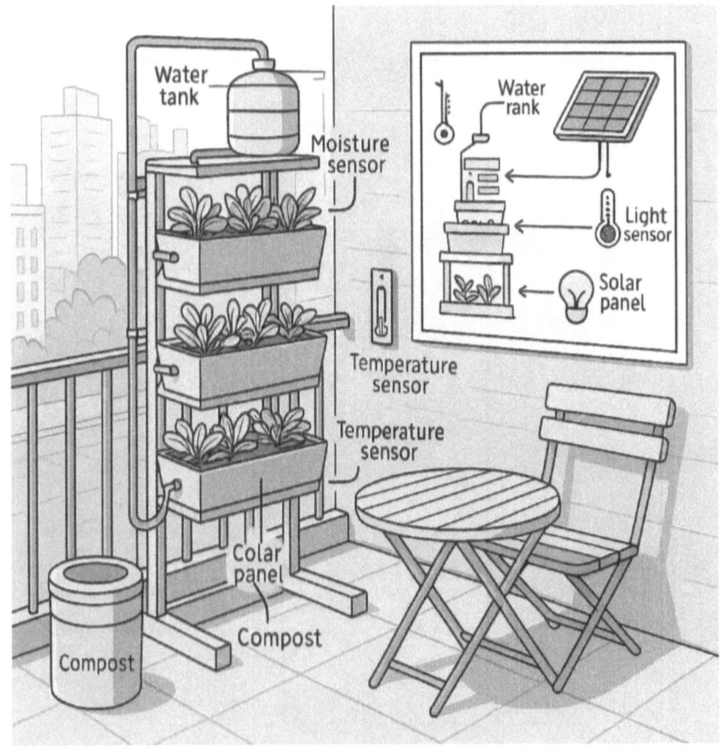

Layout of the Garden

The Arduino Uno is usually mounted near the base or on a side panel of the vertical garden or planting unit.

Connections:

- Soil Moisture Sensors → Connected to analog pins (e.g., A0, A1) and GND/VCC.
- Water Pump/Drip Irrigation System → Connected through a relay module to one of the digital output pins.
- Light Sensor (Optional) → Connected to an analog input pin.
- Power Source → Either via USB cable or an external 9V battery pack connected to the power jack.

Data Display (Optional):

If there's an LCD screen (e.g., 16x2 LCD), it would be wired to the digital pins with a potentiometer to control brightness.

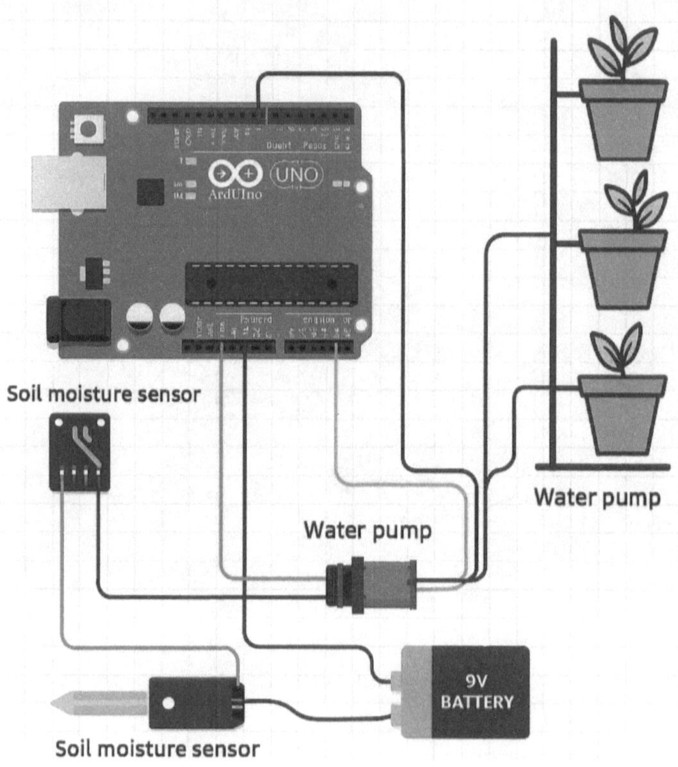

TinkerCad Design Simulation

Appendix C

Sample Lesson Plan – Introduction to Drone Technology

Title: Eyes in the Sky – Exploring Drones and Their Real-World Use
　　Grade Level: 6–8
Duration: 2 sessions (45 minutes each)
Subject Integration: Science, ICT, Geography, Ethics
　　Learning Objectives:

- Understand what drones are and how they work
- Identify key components of a drone (propellers, sensors, motors, etc.)
- Explore real-world applications: agriculture, delivery, rescue missions
- Practice coding simple flight paths (using Tello EDU or DroneBlocks)
- Discuss ethical implications of drone use (privacy, safety)

　　Materials Needed:

- Mini drones (e.g., Tello EDU)
- Tablets with DroneBlocks app
- Whiteboard & markers
- Printed drone diagram handouts
- Access to a large open space (or simulation mode if indoors)

　　Session 1 – Drone Discovery
　　1. Hook:
Show a short video of drones in action (rescuing people, planting trees, filming nature). Ask:
"Where do you think drones help us most?"

2. Direct Instruction:

Introduce drones – parts, mechanics, flight stabilization. Use a balsa model to compare basic flight principles.

3. Activity:

Students label a drone diagram and match each part with its function.

4. Exit Ticket:

Draw or write one way drones are making the world better.

Session 2 – Code & Conscience

1. Coding Flight Paths:

Use the DroneBlocks app to create a simple 5-step flight path. Students test indoors or simulate it.

2. Ethical Corner:

Debate in pairs: "Should drones be allowed to fly over schools?"

Key discussion points: data privacy, surveillance, regulation.

3. Reflection:

Students complete a journal prompt:

"If I could invent a drone for good, what would it do?"

Assessment:

- Participation in coding and discussion
- Accurate drone part labeling
- Reflection journal or group presentation

Drone Curriculum Map (Ages 8–16)

105

Age Group	Key Focus	Core Activities	Subjects Integrated	Learning Outcomes
8–10 (*Junior Explorers*)	Curiosity & Observation	- Build paper & balsa gliders - Observe flight patterns - Discuss forces of flight	Science, Art, English	Understand lift, gravity; Describe how a glider moves; Use descriptive language
11–13 (*Young Coders*)	Coding & Exploration	- Fly beginner drones (Tello) - Use block-based coding - Create mini obstacle courses	Science, ICT, Math	Write basic flight algorithms; Measure distance/time; Test and refine paths
14–16 (*Drone Designers*)	Design & Application	- CAD design glider parts - Assemble programmable drones - Simulate real-world missions (rescue, delivery)	Physics, Computer Science, Geography	Build working drone kits; Map flight paths; Analyze mission success factors

Appendix D : Printable Student Resources

The following printable worksheets and posters are included to support learning, reflection, and digital literacy in the classroom. These resources can be photocopied, printed, or shared with students to deepen their engagement in digital citizenship, STEM exploration, and reflective practices.

How to Access:

Each printable is available for download. Simply scan the QR code provided below or visit the designated link to access and print.

Included Printables:

- Weekly Tech Reflection -A guided sheet for students to reflect on their digital behavior, tools used, and challenges faced.
- Weekly Growth Journal Prompts - Prompts for students to think critically about their learning journey, helping foster a growth mindset.
- STEM Challenge Template -A space for students to plan, implement, and reflect on hands-on projects and experiments.
- Screen Time Log - A weekly tracker that helps students categorize and monitor their screen use: education, entertainment, gaming, and social media.
- Problem-Solving Steps Poster - A printable poster/checklist guiding students through a step-by-step problem-solving process.
- Internet Safety Scenario Cards - Short, discussion-based scenarios that encourage students to think about online safety and responsible decision-making.
- Failure Board: Heroic Attempt of the Week - A celebration of effort and learning from mistakes, spotlighting student persistence.
- Digital Citizenship Oath - A pledge for students to commit to respectful and responsible online behavior. Ideal for classroom display.

- Digital Footprint Tracker- A visual template helping students map and analyze their online presence and visibility.
- Create a Digital Avatar - A worksheet for students to design their online persona and reflect on the values it represents.

Download All Printables:

Scan the QR code below to access the full printable pack in high-resolution format.

Appendix E. Glossary Of Terms

- Algorithmic Bias – Systemic unfairness in code due to biased data or assumptions.
- Artificial Intelligence (AI) – A branch of computer science that simulates human intelligence through machines, enabling tasks like learning, reasoning, and decision-making.
- Autonomous Robot – A robot that can perform tasks without human intervention, often using sensors and pre-programmed logic.
- Debugging – The process of identifying and correcting errors or bugs in a computer program.
- Digital Citizenship – The responsible and ethical use of technology, especially in online environments.
- Digital Footprint – The trail of data you leave behind when interacting online, including social media posts, website visits, and shared files.
- Drone (UAV) – An Unmanned Aerial Vehicle, often used in education to teach physics, coding, or environmental applications.
- Growth Mindset – The belief that abilities and intelligence can be developed through effort, persistence, and learning from failure.
- Internet Safety – Practices that protect users from threats online, including privacy breaches, cyberbullying, and malware.
- Line Following Robot – A robot that uses sensors to detect and follow a line on the ground, commonly used in beginner robotics lessons.
- Machine Learning – A subfield of AI where computers learn from data to improve performance on a task without being explicitly programmed for every scenario.
- Oath Ceremony (Digital) – A symbolic classroom activity where students commit to ethical digital behavior through a shared

pledge.

- Obstacle Detection – A feature in robotics that enables a machine to sense and avoid barriers using ultrasonic, IR, or visual sensors.
- Python – A high-level programming language known for its readability, often used in robotics and AI education.
- Sensors – Devices that detect and respond to physical inputs like light, distance, or sound, enabling robots to perceive their environment.
- Simulations – The use of computer programs to model real-world systems, often used in cybersecurity drills or science education.
- Thrust (Drone) – The upward force that allows a drone to lift off and stay airborne, counteracting gravity.
- Voice Command Integration – The ability of a system or robot to interpret and respond to human speech, typically powered by AI.
- Virtual Collaboration – Working together online across different locations and time zones using digital tools like video calls, cloud apps, and shared documents.
- Values-Driven Coding – An approach where ethical questions and real-world impact are considered during programming.

Appendix F: Recommended Readings

1. AI 2041 by Kai-Fu Lee – A visionary exploration of how AI might reshape our world.
2. The Future of Learning – OECD Reports – Global insights on the evolution of education and technology.
3. TED Talk: The Child-Driven Education by Sugata Mitra – A revolutionary view on self-organized learning environments.
4. UN SDG Classroom Resources – Tools and content for integrating sustainability goals into your curriculum.
5. Common Sense Media Digital Citizenship Curriculum – Free, grade-wise digital citizenship resources for educators.

Let this appendix be your sandbox—where ideas grow, courage blooms, and innovation never stops.

www.ingramcontent.com/pod-product-compliance
Lightning Source LLC
Chambersburg PA
CBHW021224130726
47988CB00002B/816